CAR FERRIES
OF THE BRITISH ISLES 1994

NICK WIDDOWS

ISBN: 1 871947 18 9
Published by Ferry Publications
Design: Bezier Design and Miles Cowsill
12 Millfields Close, Kilgetty,
Pembrokeshire, SA68 0SA
Tel: (0834) 813991 Fax: (0834) 814484

Contents

Stena Invicta (Mike Louagie)

Introduction

This is the seventh edition of this book, the first of which was published in 1983. This year's issue, sponsored by *P&O European Ferries*, adds freight only operators running to Ireland and the near Continent (deep sea and Mediterranean operators are not included) as well as showing additional information about each operator and their services.

For the first time I have split the listing of companies and vessels into five. Section 1 lists operators which provide passenger and car services between the Great Britain and Ireland and the Continent, between Britain and Ireland and services from the Channel Islands and Isle of Man. Section 2 lists 'fast ferry' operations and Section 3 domestic operations – island and estuarial. Section 4 lists freight only operators and any freight only vessels operated by companies listed in Section 1. Section 5 lists other vehicle ferries. The distinction between a freight and passenger vessel can, in reality, be rather fine. I have regarded all vessels operating on services which are advertised as being available to the public and their vehicles as passenger vessels and these are listed in Section 1. This applies even if the vessel is primarily a freight vessel and if the sort of vehicle conveyed is restricted eg caravans only. Conversely, where a few passengers are carried on freight vessels on a 'cruise' basis, such vessels are regarded as freight vessels. It must be emphasised that the freight ferry scene is even more volatile than the passenger scene so any fleet list can only be a snapshot at a point in time.

A glossary of ships' names (where the derivation is not obvious or contrived) is also included and vessels whose entry to into service is very close to publication date are listed in the main part if the text, rather than in the 'under construction' section of each company's entry.

Whilst I have gone to great lengths to ensure that the facts contained here are correct, neither the publishers nor I can accept any responsibility for errors contained herein. We would, however, appreciate comments from readers, which we will endeavour to incorporate in the next edition which will be published in early 1995.

The publication of this book coincides with the opening of the Channel Tunnel. Whilst the exact impact of this is impossible to predict, there is little doubt that there will be an impact. However, it is also certain that ferries of various shapes and sizes will continue to play an important role in the life of our islands and continue to provide much interest for both the professional and the enthusiast alike.

I would like to thank all those in the various ferry companies who have helped in the preparation of this book and also others who have contributed – in particular Miles Cowsill and John Hendy of Ferry Publications.

February 1994
Whitstable, Kent

Nick Widdows

FERRY
Publications

Foreword

By Graeme Dunlop, Chairman,
P&O Ferries Limited

Since the last edition of this book was published two years ago, the ferry industry has experienced many changes - both within itself and in the markets which it operates. There is no doubt that the next couple of years will see even greater developments. It is an exciting and challenging time for us all.

The introduction to that previous edition said it would be the last to be published before the opening of the Channel Tunnel. Well, the author did not quite get that right, but after several delays the fixed link is now (almost) with us. Many words have been uttered about the impact of this new transport system upon the ferry industry, but it will be some time yet before a true picture emerges. What is certain is that all ferry routes between the British Isles and Continental Europe will, to one degree or another, be affected.

The ferry operators have had plenty of time to prepare to meet this new challenge and while it has to be conceded that the tunnel has probably increased the speed of change, the revolution which has largely transformed the ferry product was already well underway before the advent of Eurotunnel. Indeed, far from being a spur to investment, the uncertainty about future traffic levels and market share has in some cases stopped investment in new tonnage which would otherwise have gone ahead to meet the demands of a growing market.

On the whole, the ferry product has never been so good as it is now. The quality of the vessels and staff, the port handling and ticketing and reservations systems are amongst the best in the world. Eurotunnel's Le Shuttle, where vehicles load onto a train for the journey, is a 19th century concept and can offer nothing that is not already provided by the ferries. It is the through train services running direct from British city to Continental city which give a taste of the 21st century. But they are not the ferries' problem, let the airlines look out for those.

Ferry operations not directly affected by the Channel Tunnel are also faced with the possibility of change. The Scottish Office has commissioned consultants to report on the way forward for the services to the Islands. This could well lead to uniformity in treatment between the Western Isles and the Orkneys and Shetlands. On the Irish Sea there is the possibility of a move in the opposite direction with the threat of subsidy from Brussels applying to the routes between Wales and Eire but not to those between Scotland and Northern Ireland.

By the time the next edition of *Car Ferries of the British Isles* is published the face of the ferry industry may be very different from today.

Graeme Dunlop, Chairman,
P&O Ferries Limited

MORE SHIPS

Five from P&O European Ferries. Five from Stena Sealink Line. Three from Hoverspeed.

MORE SAILINGS

Up to 140 sailings between Dover – Calais round the clock, six an hour at peak times.

MORE SPACE

The large ferries on the Dover – Calais route can accommodate over 2,000 passengers and 650 cars.

MORE FACILITIES

Streamlined fast-loading systems at Dover and Calais. On-board duty and tax-free shopping, restaurants, bars, lounges, business class, children's play areas and sun-decks.

MORE EXPERIENCE

No one has more experience in Drive On, Drive Off service than Dover.

MOREOVER IT'S DOVER

PORT OF
DOVER

YOU'RE MUCH BETTER OFF ON TOP

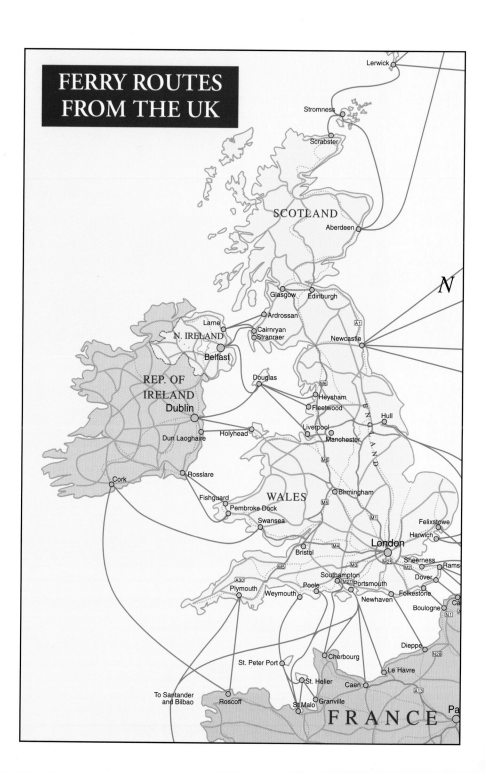

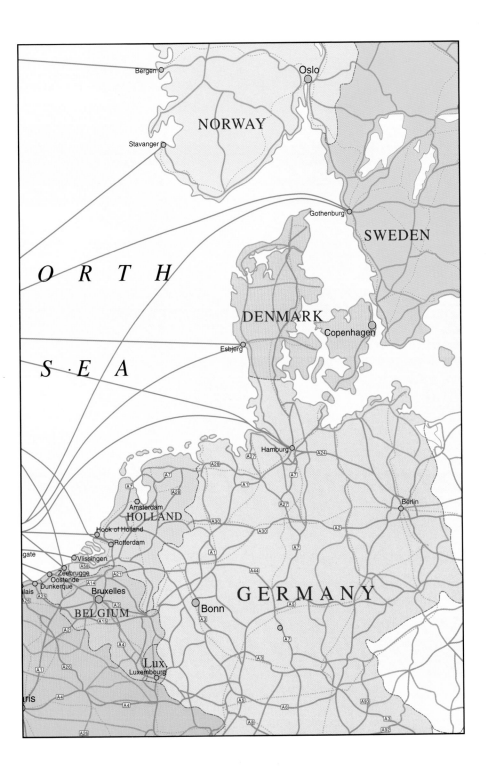

NOTES

Company information This section gives general information regarding to status of the company ie nationality, whether it is public or private section and whether it is part of a larger group.

Management The managing director and marketing director or manager of each company is listed. Where these posts do not exist, other equivalent people are listed. Where only initials are given, that person is, as far as is know, male.

Address This is the address of the company's administrative headquarters. In the case of some international companies, a British and overseas address is given.

Telephone Numbers Numbers are expressed as follows: +<*number*> (this is the international dialling code which is dialled in combination with the number dialled to gain access to international calls (010 in UK); it is not used for calling within the country), (<*number*>) (this is the internal STD number – it is not dialled when calling from another country (not all countries have this)), <*number*> (this is the rest of the number including, where appropriate, the area dialling code). Fax numbers are also quoted as are Telex numbers; it should be noted that many operators no longer use this service, its role having largely been taken over by fax.

Routes operated After each route there are, in brackets, details of **1**: normal journey time, **2**: regular vessel(s) used on the route (number as in list of vessels) and **3**: frequencies. Please note that frequencies can vary over the year. Freight operations are often restricted at weekends.

List of vessels

NO	NAME	YEAR BUILT	NUMBER OF PASSENGERS				VEHICLE DECK ACCESS*		FLAG‡
1	NAME	*26433t	87	22k	2290P	650C	100L	BA2	Town, GE	GB

(diagram labels:)
- NAME → NAME
- GROSS TONNAGE
- SERVICE SPEED (KNOTS)
- VEHICLE DECK CAPACITY†
- WHERE BUILT‡

† The following abbreviations are used:

C = Cars, L = Lorries (15m), T = Trailers (12m), R = Rail wagons, – = No figure quoted, p = passenger only vessel, c = approximate.

* The following abbreviations are used:

B = Bow, A = Aft, S = Side, Q = Quarterdeck, R = Slewing ramp, 2 = Two decks can be loaded at the same time, C = Cars must be crane loaded aboard, t = turntable ferry.

‡ The following abbreviations are used:

AL = Australia	FA = Faroes	IM = Isle of Man	PO = Poland
BA = Bahamas	FI = Finlands	IT = Italy	RO = Romania
BD = Bermuda	FR = France	JA = Japan	SI = Singapore
BE = Belgium	GB = Great Britain	LX = Luxembourg	SK = South Korea
CH = China	GE = Germany	NL = Netherlands	SW = Sweden
CR = Croatia	GI = Gibraltar	NO = Norway	YU = Yugoslavia
CY = Cyprus	GR = Greece	PA = Panama	
DK = Denmark	IC = Iceland	PL = Portugal	

In the notes ships are in CAPITAL LETTERS, shipping lines are in *italics*.

Capacity In this book, capacities shown are the maxima. Sometimes vessels operate at less than their maximum passenger capacity due to reduced crewing or to operating on a route on which they are not permitted to operate above a certain level. Car and lorry/trailer capacities are the maximum for either type. The two figures are not directly comparable; some parts of a vessel may allow cars on two levels to occupy the space that a trailer or lorry occupies on one level, some may not. Also some parts of a vessel many only be accessible to cars. All figures have to be fairly approximate.

Ownership The ownership of many vessels is very complicated. Some are actually owned by finance companies and banks, some by subsidiary companies of the shipping lines, some by subsidiary companies of a holding company of which the shipping company is also a subsidiary and some by companies which are jointly owned by the shipping company and other interests like a bank, set up specifically to own one ship or group of ships. In all these cases the vessel is technically chartered to the shipping company. However, in this book, only those vessels chartered from one shipping company to another or from a ship owning company unconnected with the shipping line, are recorded as being on charter. Vessels are listed under the current operator rather than the owner. Charter is 'bareboat' (ie without crew) unless otherwise stated.

Gross Registered Tonnage This is a measure of enclosed capacity rather than weight, based on a formula of one gross ton = 100 cubic feet. Even small alterations can alter the gross tonnage. Before 1982 car decks were not included but all vessels laid down since 1982 have been measured by a new system which includes enclosed vehicle decks as enclosed space, thereby considerably increasing the tonnage of car ferries. This includes some rebuilt vessels such as *P&O European Ferries'* PRIDE OF HAMPSHIRE. All vessels measured by the new system are indicated with an asterisk (*). Tonnages quoted here are, where possible, those given by the shipping companies themselves.

ACKNOWLEDGEMENTS

The following people are gratefully thanked for their assistance with this publication:- Ian Todd and Dave Wilson (P&O European Ferries),Toby Oliver (Brittany Ferries), Jane Rees (DFDS), Walter Bowie (Caledonian MacBrayne), Barry Mitchell, Jack Phelan, Mike Louagie, Maritime Photographic, Lawrence MacDuff, Ian Smith (Bezier Design), Foto Flite, Harcourt Litho and Pat Somner (Ferry Publications).

SECTION 1 – NORTH SEA, ENGLISH CHANNEL AND IRISH SEA PASSENGER OPERATORS

B&I LINE

THE COMPANY *B&I Line plc* is an Irish Republic private sector company, part of the *Irish Continental Group*.

MANAGEMENT Group Managing Director: Eamon Rothwell, **Group Marketing Manager:** Frank Carey.

ADDRESS B&I Ferryport, Alexandra Road, DUBLIN 1, Republic of Ireland.

TELEPHONE Administration: +353 (0)1 878 8007, **Reservations:** *Dublin* +353 (0)1 504333, *Cork* +353 (0)21 504333, *London:* +44 (0)71-734 4681, +44 (0)71-734 7512, *Manchester:* +44 (0)51-227 3131, **Fax:** *Dublin* +353 (0)1 677 8145, *Cork* +353 (0)21 504651.

ROUTES OPERATED Dublin – Holyhead (3 hrs 30 mins; *(2)*; 2 per day). Rosslare – Pembroke Dock (4 hrs 15 mins; *(1)*; 2 per day).

VESSELS

1	ISLE OF INISHMORE	6807t	81	20k	1500P	326C	39T	BA	Cork, IR	IR
2	ISLE OF INNISFREE	*19763t	86	19.4k	2000P	330C	48T	BA	Nakskov, DK	BD

Isle of Inishmore (Miles Cowsill)

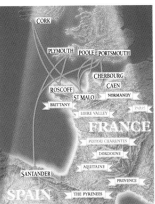

ISLE OF INISHMORE Built as the LEINSTER for *B&I Line* for the Dublin – Liverpool service. Between 1982 and 1988 she operated between Dublin and both Liverpool and Holyhead. After 1988 she operated on the Dublin – Holyhead service. In 1993 she was renamed ISLE OF INISHMORE and transferred to the Rosslare – Pembroke Dock route.

ISLE OF INNISFREE Built as the NIELS KLIM for *DSB (Danish State Railways)* for their service between Århus (Jutland) and Kalundborg (Sealand). In 1990 she was purchased by *Stena Line* of Sweden and renamed the STENA NAUTICA. In 1992 she was chartered to *B&I Line*, renamed the ISLE OF INNISFREE and introduced onto the Rosslare – Pembroke Dock service, replacing the MUNSTER (8093t, 1970). In 1993 she was transferred to the Dublin – Holyhead service. She is sister of *Stena Sealink Line's* STENA INVICTA.

BRITTANY FERRIES

THE COMPANY *Brittany Ferries* is the trading name of BAI SA, a French private sector company and the operating arm of the *Brittany Ferries* group. The UK operations are run by *BAI (UK) Ltd*, a UK private sector company, wholly owned by the *Brittany Ferries Group*.

MANAGEMENT Group Managing Director: Christian Michielini, Managing Director UK & Ireland: Ian Carruthers, Marketing Director: David Longden.

ADDRESS Millbay Docks, PLYMOUTH, Devon PL1 3EW.

TELEPHONE Administration: +44 (0)705 827701, Reservations: *Portsmouth:* +44 (0)705 827701, *Plymouth:* +44 (0)752 221321, Fax: +44 (0)705 811053, Telex: 86878.

ROUTES OPERATED Roscoff – Plymouth (6hrs (day), 5 hrs 30 mins – 7 hrs 30 mins (night); *(5,6)*; up to 3 per day), Plymouth – Santander (Spain) (spring, summer, autumn only) (23 hrs – 24 hrs; *(6)*; 2 per week), Portsmouth – Santander (Spain) (winter only) (29 hrs – 33 hrs; *(1,6)*; 1 per week), Roscoff – Cork (14hrs; *(3,6)*; up to 2 per week), St Malo – Cork (18hrs; *(3)*; 1 per week), St Malo – Portsmouth St (8 hrs 45 mins (day), 9 hrs 30 mins – 10 hrs (night); *(1)*; 1 per day), Caen (Ouistreham) – Portsmouth (6 hrs (day), 6 hrs – 7 hrs (night); *(1)*; 3 per day). St Malo – Poole (8 hrs; *(3)*; 4 per week).

VESSELS

1	BRETAGNE	*23000t	89	21k	2030P	580C	40L	BA	St Nazaire, FR	FR
2	DUC DE NORMANDIE	9355t	78	21k	1500P	350C	44T	BA	Heusden, NL	FR
3	DUCHESSE ANNE	6812t	79	20k	1300P	290C	39T	BA	Cork, IR	FR
4	NORMANDIE	*27000t	92	20k	2263P	630C	66T	BA	Turku, FI	FR
5	QUIBERON	8441t	75	20k	1302P	300C	35L	BA2	Rendsburg, GE	FR
6	VAL DE LOIRE	*31395t	87	21k	1800P	550C	114T	BA	Bremerhaven, GE	SW

BRETAGNE Built for the *Brittany Ferries* for their Plymouth – Santander and Cork – Roscoff services (with two trips per week between Plymouth and Roscoff). In 1993 she was transferred to the St Malo – Portsmouth service. She continues to operate the Portsmouth – Santander route at some times during the winter.

DUC DE NORMANDIE Built as the PRINSES BEATRIX for *Stoomvaart Maatschappij Zeeland (Zeeland Steamship Company)* of The Netherlands for their Hoek van Holland – Harwich service. In September 1985 sold to *Brittany Ferries* and chartered back to *SMZ*, continuing to operate for them until the introduction of the KONINGIN BEATRIX in May 1986. In June 1986 delivered to *Brittany Ferries* and inaugurated the Portsmouth – Caen service.

DUCHESSE ANNE Built as the CONNACHT for *B&I Line* and initially used on the Cork – Swansea (from spring 1979, Cork – Pembroke Dock) service. In late 1980 she was transferred to the Dublin – Liverpool service – initially with the MUNSTER (4230t, 1968) and from summer 1981 with the new LEINSTER. Subsequently she also operated between Dublin and Holyhead. In January 1988 she was moved to the reinstated Rosslare – Pembroke Dock service. In late 1988 she was sold to *Brittany Ferries*, renamed the DUCHESSE ANNE, re-registered in France and, in 1989, introduced onto the Portsmouth – St Malo service. In 1993 moved to operate additional Roscoff – Plymouth services, an additional Roscoff – Cork service and inaugurate a St Malo – Cork service. In summer 1994 she will inaugurate a new St Malo – Poole service, which will replace her Plymouth – Roscoff sailings.

NORMANDIE Built for *Brittany Ferries* for the Portsmouth – Caen route.

QUIBERON Ordered by *Lion Ferry AB* of Sweden. The contract was sold to *Svenska Lastbils AB (Svelast)* of Sweden (a subsidiary of *Statens Järnvägar (SJ), Swedish State Railways)* before delivery and she was delivered to them as the NILS DACKE. She was initially chartered to *Svenska Rederi AB Öresund* (another SJ subsidiary) for their service between Malmö (Sweden) and Travemünde (Germany). Sister vessel the GUSTAV VASA (now NORRÖNA of *Smyril Line*) was owned by *Lion Ferry AB* of Sweden and was also chartered to *SRÖ*. In 1976, *Svelast* took over the marketing of the service and it was operated under the name *Malmö-Travemünde Line,* with *Lion Ferry AB* operating it as agents. Later in 1976, *Svelast* and *Linjebuss International* (a subsidiary of *Stockholms Rederi AB Svea*) formed a jointly owned subsidiary called *Saga-Linjen* and *Lion Ferry AB* continued as administrative operator. In 1981 a joint marketing agreement was reached with the rival German owned *TT Line,* (running between Travemünde and Trelleborg (Sweden)) and the two services were marketed as *TT-Saga Line.* In April 1982 the NILS DACKE was chartered to *Brittany Ferries* with an option to purchase. She was renamed the QUIBERON and placed on the Plymouth – Santander and Cork – Roscoff services; she also operates between Plymouth and Roscoff. The GUSTAV VASA continued as sole vessel on the Malmö – Travemünde route for a further year until the service was withdrawn. The QUIBERON was purchased by *Brittany Ferries* in 1984 and re-registered in France. Following the delivery of the BRETAGNE in July 1989, she was transferred to the Plymouth – Roscoff service.

VAL DE LOIRE Built as the NILS HOLGERSSON for *TT Line* of Sweden and Germany (jointly owned) for their service between Travemünde and Trelleborg. In 1991 purchased by *Brittany Ferries* for entry into service in spring 1993. After a major rebuild, she was renamed the VAL DE LOIRE and introduced onto the Plymouth-Santander and Roscoff-Plymouth/Cork service. She operates on the Portsmouth – Santander and Portsmouth – Caen routes in the winter.

Val de Loire (Miles Cowsill)

Quiberon (John Hendy)

COLOR LINE

THE COMPANY *Color Line* is the trading name of *Norway Line Ltd*, which is owned by *Color Line A/S*, a Norwegian limited company. Until 1991 it traded as *Norway Line*.

MANAGEMENT Manager: Dag Romslo, **Sales Manager:** Mike Wood.

ADDRESS Tyne Commission Quay, NORTH SHIELDS, Tyne and Wear NE29 6EA.

TELEPHONE Administration: +44 (0)91-296 1313. **Reservations:** +44 (0)91-296 1313. **Fax:** +44 (0)91-296 1540. **Telex:** 537275.

ROUTES OPERATED Bergen – Stavanger – Newcastle – Bergen (triangular service – some services operate Bergen – Stavanger – Newcastle – Stavanger – Bergen) (Bergen – Stavanger (6 hrs), Stavanger – Newcastle (direct 19 hrs, via Bergen 29 hrs 30 mins), Bergen – Newcastle (direct 21 hrs 15 mins, via Stavanger 25 hrs; *(1)*; 3 sailings Norway – UK per week).

VESSEL

VENUS	*13286t	74	21.5k	1040P	270C	38L	BA	Turku, FI	NO

VENUS Built as the PRINSESSAN BIRGITTA for *Göteborg – Frederikshavnlinjen* and *Ragne Rederi AB* of Sweden (trading as *Sessan Line*) for their alternate day Göteborg – Travemünde service. The company was taken over by rival *Stena Line AB* in 1981 and later that year she was transferred to their Göteborg – Kiel route, the Travemünde route becoming freight only. In 1982 a new PRINSESSAN BIRGITTA was delivered (see the STENA NORMANDY, *Stena Sealink Line*) and she was renamed the STENA SCANDINAVICA. She remained on the Göteborg – Kiel route until 1987 when she was replaced by the new STENA GERMANICA (24967t, 1987). During summer 1987 she was chartered to *Cotunav*, the Tunisian state shipping concern, and used on their service between Tunis and Marseilles (France) and Genova (Italy). In early 1988 a new STENA SCANDINAVICA, sister vessel of the STENA GERMANICA, was delivered and she was further renamed the SCANDINAVICA. In June 1988 she was taken on four months charter by *Sealink British Ferries* and used on additional sailings between Dover (Eastern Docks) and Calais (passenger and freight services) and Zeebrugge (freight only services). In 1989, after further charter to *Cotunav*, being renamed the TARAK L, she was sold to *Norway Line*. In 1990 she was renamed the VENUS, re-registered in Norway and took over the Bergen/Stavanger – Newcastle service from the JUPITER (9499t, 1966).

Color Line also operate other vessels on routes which do not serve the UK. Those used on services between Norway and Denmark are: JUPITER (11344t, 1973) (ex BOLERO 1990, ex SCANDINAVICA 1981, ex BOLERO 1978), CHRISTIAN IV (14990t, 1982) (ex BAYARD 1990, ex OLAU BRITANNIA 1990), SKAGEN (7570t, 1975 (rebuilt 1982)) (ex BORGEN 1990). Those used on the Oslo – Kiel service are: KRONPRINS HARALD (31914t, 1987) and PRINCESSE RAGNHILDE (38500t, 1981 (rebuilt 1992)).

CONDOR

THE COMPANY *Condor* is a Channel Islands private sector company, 80% owned by *TNT* of Australia.

MANAGEMENT Managing Director: Bob Adams, **Marketing Manager:** Sam Spindlow.

ADDRESS PO Box 10, Commodore House, Bulwer Avenue, St Sampsons, GUERNSEY, Channel Islands GY1 3AF.

TELEPHONE Administration: +44 (0)481 48771 **Reservations:** +44 (0)481 726121. **Fax:** +44 (0)481 45049.

ROUTES OPERATED Weymouth – St Peter Port (Guernsey) – St Helier (Jersey) (Weymouth – Guernsey: 4hrs 30 mins (day), 9 hrs (night), Guernsey – Jersey: 2 hrs, Weymouth – Jersey (overall): 11 hrs10 mins (night), 7 hrs 50 mins (day); *(1)*; 1 per day).

VESSEL

HAVELET	3382t	77	19k	500P	200C	37L	BA2	Bergen, NO	BA

HAVELET Built as the CORNOUAILLES for *Brittany Ferries* and used mainly on their Plymouth – Roscoff service. In 1984 she was chartered to *SNCF* for use on their Dieppe – Newhaven service. This charter terminated at the end of 1985 and she was transferred to *Truckline Ferries*. From January 1986 she operated on their Poole – Cherbourg freight only service and then, in April, she inaugurated the Portsmouth – Caen service for *Brittany Ferries* on a freight only basis. In June she returned to *Truckline Ferries* and inaugurated a car and passenger service between Poole and Cherbourg. Until 1989 she operated between Poole and Cherbourg all year round, conveying passengers between April and October only. In 1989 she was renamed the HAVELET and sold *Channel Island Ferries*, holding company of *British Channel Island Ferries*, operating between Poole and the Channel Islands. It was intended that, in 1993, she would be used in a freight only role; however, due to the level of demand it was decided to allow her to carry passengers and she was crewed accordingly. In 1994, *British Channel Island Ferries* ceased operations and she was chartered to *Condor* to operate between Weymouth and the Channel Islands.

EMERAUDE LINES

THE COMPANY *Emeraude Lines* is a French private sector company.

MANAGEMENT Commercial Manager (St Malo): Jean-Luc Griffon, **Managing Director (Jersey):** Gordon Forrest.

ADDRESS PO Box 16, 35401, St Malo, France.

TELEPHONE Administration & Reservations: *St Malo:* +33 99 40 48 40, *Jersey* +44 (0)534 66566, **Fax:** *St Malo:* +33 99 81 28 73, *Jersey* +44 (0)534 68741.

ROUTES OPERATED Until 14 May 1994 only St Malo (France) – St Helier (Jersey) (2 hrs 30 mins – 3 hrs; *1*); 2 per day). For service from 15 May 1994 see Section 2.

VESSEL

SOLIDOR 2	2158t	77	15k	600P	90C	13L	BA	Hoogezand, NL	FR

SOLIDOR 2 Built as the LANGELAND II (registered in Denmark as the LANGELAND TO) for *Langeland – Kiel Linien* of Denmark for their service between Bagenkop (Langeland, Denmark) and Kiel (Germany). In 1989 she was purchased by *Emeraude Lines* and replaced the SOLIDOR (1000t, 1965) (the same vessel she replaced in 1977 when new since the SOLIDOR was previously the LANGELAND). To be withdrawn in May 1994 and replaced by the EMERAUDE.

Venus (Color Line)

Saint Patrick II (Miles Cowsill)

· *ferry* ENJOYABLE ·

For many people, sailing to the Isle of Man is the <u>only</u> way to travel.

Relaxing, comfortable, reassuringly easy on the pocket...and with the extra advantage of being able to take the car.

Our ships are modern, spacious and equipped with everything from restaurants and bars, to shops, video lounges and safe playing areas for children.

The Steam Packet operate year round sailings to the Isle of Man from Heysham and Liverpool with seasonal services from Fleetwood, Belfast, Dublin and Ardrossan.

Next time you're travelling to the Island, sail with the Steam Packet for a **ferry** refreshing experience.

(0624) 661661

Isle of Man
Steam Packet Company
P.O. Box 5, Douglas,
Isle of Man

HEYSHAM • LIVERPOOL • FLEETWOOD • BELFAST • DUBLIN • ARDROSSAN • TO THE ISLE OF MAN

ISLE OF MAN STEAM PACKET COMPANY

THE COMPANY *The Isle of Man Steam Packet Company,* is an Isle of Man registered company. A 41% share in the company is owned by *Sea Containers.*

MANAGEMENT Managing Director: David Dixon, **Passenger Manager:** Richard Kirkman.

ADDRESS PO Box 5, Imperial Buildings, DOUGLAS, Isle of Man.

TELEPHONE Administration: +44 (0)624 623344, **Reservations:** +44 (0)624 661661, **Fax:** +44 (0)624 661065, **Telex:** 627741.

ROUTES OPERATED *All year:* Douglas (Isle of Man) – Heysham (3 hrs 45 mins; *(1,2)*; up to 2 per day), Douglas – Liverpool (4 hrs, 30 mins; *(1,2)*; irregular). *Summer only:* Douglas – Fleetwood (3 hrs 30 mins; *(1)*; 1 per week), Douglas – Belfast (4 hrs 30 mins; *(1)*; 2 per week), Douglas – Dublin (4hrs 45 mins; *(1)*; 2 per week), Douglas – Ardrossan (in association with *Caledonian MacBrayne*) (8 hrs; *(Calmac vessel)*; weekly).

VESSELS

| 1 | KING ORRY | 4649t | 75 | 19.5k | 1100P | 170C | 34T | AS | Genova, IT | BA |
| 2 | LADY OF MANN | 3177t | 76 | 21k | 1000P | 130C | 0L | S | Troon, GB | IM |

KING ORRY Built as the SAINT ELOI for *ALA* (Société Anonyme de Navigation Angleterre Lorraine-Alsace), a wholly owned subsidiary of *Sealink UK Ltd* registered in France, for the Dover – Dunkerque train ferry service. Although built in 1973 she did not enter service until 1975. She ceased carrying passengers and accompanied cars in September 1985. Replaced on the Dunkerque Ouest – Dover service by the NORD PAS-DE-CALAIS in May 1988. In summer 1988 she resumed passenger service and operated sailings primarily for rail connected foot passengers between Calais and Dover (Western Docks) on charter to *Sealink – SNCF*. In summer 1989 she was renamed the CHANNEL ENTENTE; she operated the same services as 1988 but for *Sealink British Ferries*. In 1990 she was purchased from *ALA*, re-registered in the Bahamas and took up service on the Douglas – Heysham service. Following a major refurbishment in the autumn 1990, she was renamed the KING ORRY.

LADY OF MANN Built for the *IOMSP*. Cars and small vans are side loaded but no RO/RO freight is conveyed. Now used on Douglas to Heysham (peak periods), Liverpool, Fleetwood, Belfast and Dublin services.

IRISH FERRIES

THE COMPANY *Irish Ferries* is the trading name of *Irish Continental Line*, an Irish Republic private sector company, part of the *Irish Continental Group*. It was originally mainly owned by the state owned *Irish Shipping* and partly by *Lion Ferry AB* of Sweden. *Lion Ferry* participation ceased in 1977 and the company was sold into the private sector in 1987.

MANAGEMENT Group Managing Director: Eamon Rothwell, **Group Marketing Director:** Frank Carey.

ADDRESS 2 Merrion Row, DUBLIN 2, Republic of Ireland.

TELEPHONE Administration: +353 (0)1 661 0714, **Reservations:** *Dublin:* +353 (0)1 661 0714, *Cork:* +353 (0)21 378111.

ROUTES OPERATED Routes operated: *All year*: Rosslare – Cherbourg (17 hrs; *(1,2)*; up to 2 per week), Rosslare – Le Havre (21 hrs; *(1,2)*; up to 3 per week), *Summer only*: Cork – Cherbourg (18 hrs 30 mins; *(1,2)*; 1 per week), Cork – Le Havre (21 hrs 30 mins; *(1,2)*; 1 per week).

VESSELS

1	SAINT KILLIAN II	10256t	73	20.5k	2000P	380C	36L	BA	Kraljevica, YU	IR
2	SAINT PATRICK II	7984t	73	20.5k	1630P	300C	31L	BA	Hamburg, GE	IR

SAINT KILLIAN II Built as the STENA SCANDINAVICA for *Stena Line AB* of Sweden for their service from Göteborg to Kiel (with a day-time return trip from Kiel to Korsør or Nyborg in Denmark and from Göteborg to Frederikshavn, Denmark). In 1978 she was purchased by *Irish Continental Line* in order to inaugurate a new service between Rosslare and Cherbourg in addition to their Rosslare – Le Havre service. She was renamed the SAINT KILLIAN. In 1980 she was chartered back to *Stena Line* for two months to operate between Göteborg and Kiel and Frederikshavn. After the 1981 summer season a new 32m section was added amidships, raising gross tonnage from 7126t to 10256t and passenger capacity from 1500 to 2000. On return to service in early 1982 she was renamed the SAINT KILLIAN II. She operates on all routes.

SAINT PATRICK II Built as the AURELLA for *SF Line* of Finland (a member of *Viking Line*) for services between Naantali (Finland), Mariehamn (Åland) and Kapellskär (Sweden). In 1982 she was acquired by *Irish Continental Line*, renamed the SAINT PATRICK II and replaced the SAINT PATRICK (5285t, 1973), which had been transferred to *Belfast Car Ferries* (an associated company which used to operate between Liverpool and Belfast) and renamed the SAINT COLUM I (5284t, 1973). She also substituted for the SAINT COLUM I on the Liverpool – Belfast service. In 1987 she was transferred to *Belfast Car Ferries* but returned to *Irish Ferries* in spring 1988 as it was not possible to find a replacement for her. She is generally not required during the winter (except when the SAINT KILLIAN II is being overhauled) and is usually chartered out. Charterers have included *B&I Line*, *North Sea Ferries*, *P&O European Ferries* and *Stena Line*.

NORSE IRISH FERRIES

THE COMPANY *Norse Irish Ferries* is a British private sector company. It started as a freight only operation but passenger facilities were established in 1992.

MANAGEMENT Managing Director: Philip Shepherd, **Marketing Manager:** Nigel Hamilton.

ADDRESS *Belfast:* Victoria Terminal 2, West Bank Road, BELFAST BT3 9JN, *Liverpool:* North Brocklebank Dock, BOOTLE, Merseyside L20 1BY.

TELEPHONE Administration: *Belfast:* +44 (0)232 779090, *Liverpool:* +44 (0)51-944 1010, **Reservations (Passenger):** *Belfast:* +44 (0)232 779090/779191, *Liverpool:* +44 (0)51-944 1010, **Fax:** *Belfast:* +44 (0)232 775520, *Liverpool:* +44 (0)51-922 0344.

ROUTE OPERATED Liverpool – Belfast (11 hrs; *(1,2)*; 1 per day).

VESSELS

1	NORSE LAGAN	*22508t	68	18.5k	200P	360C	140T	AS2	Lauzon, CD	NL
2	NORSE MERSEY	*20914t	69	18k	144P	–	200T	AS	Helsinki, FI	BA

Norland (John Hendy)

King Orry (Miles Cowsill)

NORSE LAGAN Built as the FREDERICK CARTER and used on freight services in Canada. In 1986 renamed the FRED and sold to *Anco Ferries* of Greece who renamed her the FLAVIA II. In 1987 chartered to *Olympic Ferries* who renamed her the ATHENIA. In 1988 renamed the THENIA and sold to *Nordö Link* of Sweden who renamed her the HANSA LINK and used her on their service between Malmö and Travemünde. During winter 1989-90 she was lengthened and an extra vehicle deck added. In 1991 chartered to *Norse Irish Ferries*, renamed the NORSE LAGAN and introduced on their Liverpool – Belfast freight service. In 1992 she began carrying cars and passengers.

NORSE MERSEY Built as the FINNCARRIER for *Finnlines* (later *Finncarriers*) of Finland for service between Finland, Denmark and Germany. In 1975 renamed the POLARIS. In 1984 sold to *Rederi AB Nordö* of Sweden to operate between Malmö (Sweden) and Travemünde (Germany) and renamed the SCANDINAVIA. In 1987 she was rebuilt to increase capacity from 122 trailers to 200 and remeasured under the new system. In 1989 the trading name of the company was changed to *Nordö Link* and she was renamed the SCANDINAVIA LINK. In 1990 she was sold to *Stena Line* of Sweden, renamed the STENA SEARIDER and used on their Göteborg (Sweden) – Travemünde service. In 1991 she was chartered out for service in the Caribbean and renamed the SEARIDER. In 1992 she was chartered to *Norse Irish Ferries* and renamed the NORSE MERSEY.

Norse Lagan (Norse Irish)

NORTH SEA FERRIES

THE COMPANY *North Sea Ferries* is a private sector international company jointly owned by *The P&O Group* of Great Britain and *Nedlloyd* of The Netherlands.

MANAGEMENT Managing Director: Russ Peters, **Marketing Managers:** *UK:* Tony Farrell, *Netherlands:* J Gijs Jordaan, *Belgium:* Christian Berkein.

ADDRESS *UK:* King George Dock, Hedon Road, HULL HU5 3NU, *Netherlands:* Beneluxhaven, Rotterdam (Europoort), Postbus 1123, 3180 Rozenburg ZH, Netherlands, *Belgium:* Leopold II Dam 13, Havendam, B-8380, Zeebrugge, Belgium.

TELEPHONE Administration: *UK:* +44 (0)482 795141, *Netherlands:* +31 (0)1819 55500, *Belgium:* +32 (0)50 54 34 11. **Reservations:** *UK:* +44 (0)482 77177, *Netherlands:* +31 (0)1819 29571, *Belgium:* +32 (0)50 54 34 30. **Fax:** *UK:* +44 (0)482 706438, *Netherlands:* +31 (0)1819 55322, *Belgium:* +32 (0)50 54 68 35, **Telex:** *UK:* 592349, *Netherlands:* 29652, *Belgium:* 81469.

ROUTES OPERATED Hull – Rotterdam (Europoort) (13 hrs; *(2,4)*; 1 per day), Hull – Zeebrugge (13 hrs 30 mins; *(1,3)*; 1 per day).

VESSELS

1	NORLAND	*26290t	74	18.5k	881P	500C	134T	A	Bremerhaven, GE	GB
2	NORSEA	*31785t	87	18.5k	1250P	850C	180T	A	Glasgow, GB	GB
3	NORSTAR	*26919t	74	18.5k	881P	500C	134T	A	Bremerhaven, GE	NL
4	NORSUN	*31598t	87	18.5k	1250P	850C	180T	A	Tsurumi, JA	NL

NORLAND Built for *North Sea Ferries* for the Hull – Rotterdam service. She is owned by *P&O*. In April 1982 she was requisitioned for the Falkland Islands Task Force by the Ministry of Defence. She took part in the invasion of the Islands, disembarking troops and equipment at San Carlos. After the cessation of hostilities she made trips to Argentina and Uruguay and was then employed on a shuttle service between Port Stanley and Ascension. She returned to Hull on 1st February 1983 and re-entered service on the Rotterdam service on 19th April. In 1987 she was 'stretched' and refurbished to a similar standard to the NORSEA. She replaced the NORWAVE (3450t, 1965) on the Hull – Zeebrugge service.

NORSEA, NORSUN Built for *North Sea Ferries* for their Hull – Rotterdam service. The NORSEA is owned by *P&O* and the NORSUN is owned by *Nedlloyd*.

NORSTAR Built for *North Sea Ferries* for the Hull – Rotterdam service. She is owned by *Nedlloyd*. In 1987 she was 'stretched' and replaced the NORWIND (3692t, 1966) on the Hull – Zeebrugge service.

OLAU LINE

THE COMPANY *Olau Line* is a private sector company owned by *OHG Olau Line (UK) AG* of Germany which is associated with *TT- Line*. The Company is named after its Danish founder Ole Lauritzen who sold the company to its present owners in 1978. The service is due to cease in May 1994.

MANAGEMENT General Manager: Case Rietkerk, **Marketing Manager:** Patrick Williams.

ADDRESS Sheerness Docks, SHEERNESS, Kent, ME12 1SN.

TELEPHONE Administration: +44 (0)795 580010. **Reservations:** +44 (0)795 666666. **Fax:** +44 (0)795 666919. **Telex:** 965605.

ROUTES OPERATED Sheerness – Vlissingen (Netherlands) (7hrs day, 8hrs 30 mins night; *(1,2)*; 2 per day).

VESSELS

OLAU BRITANNIA	*33336t	90	21k	1600P	575C	118T	BA	Bremerhaven, GE	GE
OLAU HOLLANDIA	*33336t	89	21k	1600P	575C	118T	BA	Bremerhaven, GE	GE

Eastern Docks, Dover (FotoFlite)

OLAU BRITANNIA Built for *Olau Line*. In May 1994 to be chartered to *P&O European Ferries* and renamed the PRIDE OF PORTSMOUTH. To be used on their Portsmouth-Le Havre service as from June 1994.

OLAU HOLLANDIA Built for *Olau Line*. In May 1994 to be chartered to *P&O European Ferries* and renamed the PRIDE OF LE HAVRE. To be used on their Portsmouth-Le Havre service as from June 1994.

Pride of Le Havre (P&O European Ferries)

OOSTENDE LINES

THE COMPANY *Oostende Lines* is the trading name of *RMT (Regie voor Maritiem Transport – Maritime Transport Authority (RTM – Regie des Transports Maritimes* in French))*, an agency of the Belgian Government. Until 1985 operations were part of the *Sealink* pool but from January 1986 services were operated as part of the *Townsend Thoresen* network and the ships received *Townsend Thoresen* orange hulls and 'TOWNSEND THORESEN' lettering. With the change to *P&O European Ferries* there was a reversion to plain hulls (albeit blue rather than the previous black) but services continued to be marketed in the UK by *P&O*. The trading name of *Dover – Ostend Line*, together with new livery and logo, was adopted in 1991. In 1994 services were transferred to Ramsgate in conjunction with *Sally Line* and the trading name changed to *Oostende Lines*.

MANAGEMENT Commercial Director: Francis Engelen.

ADDRESS Natienkaai 5, 8400 Oostende, Belgium.

TELEPHONE Administration: +32 (0)59 55 91 11, **Reservations:** Belgium: +32 (0)59 55 99 55, **Fax:** *Admin:* +32 (0)59 80 86 56, *Reservations:* +32 (0)59 80 94 17, U.K: See *Sally Line.*

ROUTE OPERATED Oostende – Ramsgate (4 hrs – 4 hrs, 45 mins; *(2,3,4)*; 6 per day).

VESSELS

1	PRINCESSE MARIE- CHRISTINE	6181t	76	22K	1200P	354C	68T	BA2	Hoboken, BE	BE
2	PRINS ALBERT	6613t	78	22k	1200P	354C	68T	BA2	Hoboken, BE	BE
3	PRINS FILIP	*28838t	91	21k	1350P	710C	145T	BAS	Temse, BE	BE
4	REINE ASTRID	5574t	75	17k	1000P	450C	66T	BA2	Bremerhaven, GE	BE

PRINCESS MARIE-CHRISTINE Built for *RMT*. During 1985 she had an extra vehicle deck added, increasing vehicle capacity. Passenger capacity was increased by 200 by the conversion of an upper deck 'garage' into passenger accommodation. Operated during the early part of 1994 whilst additional dredging took place to enable PRINS FILIP to use the port. Now a spare vessel and for sale.

PRINS ALBERT Built for *RMT*. During 1986 she had an additional vehicle deck added.

PRINS FILIP Built for *RMT (Dover – Ostend Line)*; Although completed in 1991 she did not enter service until May 1992.

REINE ASTRID Built as the STENA NORDICA for *Stena Line AB* of Sweden, one of four similar vessels built for chartering. The other three were the STENA NORMANDICA (now WASA SUN of *Silja Line* after having been with *Sealink* for 11 years, the last five as the ST BRENDAN), the STENA NAUTICA (now the CORSICA MARINA II of *Corsica Ferries*) and the STENA ATLANTICA (now the SARDINIA VERA of *Sardinia Ferries*). In 1978 she was chartered to *Soutos Hellas* of Greece, renamed the HELLAS and used on services between Volas (Greece) and Latakia (Syria). In 1979 she resumed her original name for a short time but later in the year she returned to *Soutos Hellas* and was again named the HELLAS. In 1980 she resumed the name STENA NORDICA again. Subsequent charters included *B&I Line* for the Rosslare – Pembroke Dock service, *CN Marine* for the service between North Sydney (Nova Scotia) and Port-aux-Basques (Newfoundland) and *Sealink UK* for the Fishguard – Rosslare service. After her return from Canada in 1981 she underwent a refit in the Clyde and then went for a further period of charter with *Soutos Hellas*. On return in 1982, she was renamed the STENA NAUTICA (taking the name of her sister vessel which had been sold to *CN Marine* of Canada and renamed the MARINE NAUTICA) and chartered to *RMT*. Ownership was transferred to a *Stena Line* subsidiary in Belgium called *Nautica (Belgium) NV* and registry was transferred to Belgium. In March 1983 she was purchased by *RMT* and renamed the REINE ASTRID. She is slower than other vessels and, when operating from Dover, was only used on Eastern Docks services.

Oostende Lines also operate two Boeing Jetfoils of 289t, built in Seattle, USA in 1981 and carrying 280 passengers between Oostende and Ramsgate. They are named the PRINCESSE CLEMENTINE and the PRINSES STEPHANIE. No cars are conveyed.

Princesse Marie-Christine (Mike Louagie)

Pride of Flanders (John Hendy)

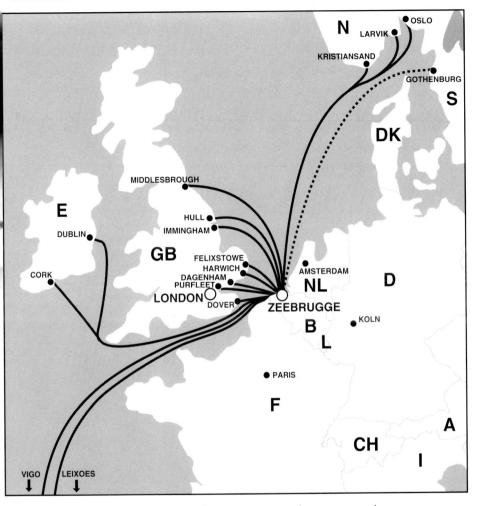

P&O EUROPEAN FERRIES

THE COMPANY *P&O European Ferries Ltd* is the trading name of *P&O European Ferries (Dover)*, *P&O European Ferries (Portsmouth)* and *P&O European Ferries (Felixstowe)*, British private sector companies, part of the *P&O Group*. These companies were, until 1987, respectively: *Townsend Car Ferries*, *Thoresen Car Ferries* and *Atlantic Steam Navigation*, all part of *European Ferries* and trading as *Townsend Thoresen*. *European Ferries* was taken over by the *P&O Group* in January 1987 and the trading name was changed in October 1987.

MANAGEMENT **Managing Director:** Graeme Dunlop, **Passenger Marketing & Sales Director:** Brian Langford.

ADDRESS Channel House, Channel View Road, DOVER, Kent CT17 9TJ.

TELEPHONE Administration: +44 (0)304 223000 **Reservations:** +44 (0)304 203388 (Portsmouth – Bilbao service: +44 (0)304 240077), **Fax:** +44 (0)304 223223, **Telex:** 965104.

ROUTES OPERATED Cairnryan – Larne (2 hrs 15 mins; *(1,12)*; up to 6 per day), Portsmouth – Cherbourg (4 hrs 45 mins (day), 8 hrs 45 mins – 9 hrs 45 mins (night); *(2,6,14)*; 3 per day), Portsmouth – Le Havre (5hrs 45 mins (day), 7 hrs – 9 hrs (night); *(9,11)*; 3 per day), Portsmouth – Bilbao (Spain) (33-34 hrs (UK-Spain), 30 hrs (Spain-UK); *(2)*; 2 per week), Dover – Calais (1 hr 15 mins; *(3,4,5,7,10)*; up 25 per day), Felixstowe – Zeebrugge (5 hrs 45 mins (day), 8 hrs (night); *(8,13)*; 2 per day).

VESSELS

1	PRIDE OF AILSA	*12503t	72	19.5k	1041P	340C	60L	BA2	Schiedam, NL	GB
2	PRIDE OF BILBAO	37583t	86	22k	2500P	600C	90T	BA	Turku, FI	BA
3	PRIDE OF BRUGES	7951t	80	23k	1326P	336C	73L	BA2	Bremerhaven, GE	GB
4	PRIDE OF BURGUNDY	*28138t	93	21k	1320P	600C	148T	BA2	Bremerhaven, GE	GB
5	PRIDE OF CALAIS	*26433t	87	22k	2290P	650C	100L	BA2	Bremerhaven, GE	GB
6	PRIDE OF CHERBOURG	6386t	76	19k	1200P	275C	26L	BA	Ålborg, DK	GB
7	PRIDE OF DOVER	*26433t	87	22k	2290P	650C	100L	BA2	Bremerhaven, GE	GB
8	PRIDE OF FLANDERS	*18732t	78	17k	688P	220C	40T	A2	Ulsan, SK	GB
9	PRIDE OF HAMPSHIRE	*14760t	75	18k	1200P	380C	50L	BA2	Ålborg, DK	GB
10	PRIDE OF KENT	*20446t	80	23k	1825P	460C	64T	BA2	Bremerhaven, GE	GB
11	PRIDE OF LE HAVRE	*14760t	75	18k	1200P	380C	50L	BA2	Ålborg, DK	GB
12	PRIDE OF RATHLIN	*12503t	73	19.5k	1035P	340C	60L	BA2	Schiedam, NL	GB
13	PRIDE OF SUFFOLK	*18732t	78	17k	688P	220C	40T	A2	Ulsan, SK	GB
14	PRIDE OF WINCHESTER	6386t	76	19k	1200P	275C	26L	BA	Ålborg, DK	GB

PRIDE OF AILSA Built as the FREE ENTERPRISE VI for Dover – Calais and Dover – Zeebrugge services. After 1980 she was generally used on the Dover – Zeebrugge service. In 1985/86 she was 'stretched' in Bremerhaven, Germany, through the placing of the existing superstructure and rear part of hull on a new front part of hull. She was renamed the PRIDE OF SANDWICH in 1988. In 1992 she was transferred to the Cairnryan – Larne route and renamed the PRIDE OF AILSA.

PRIDE OF BILBAO Built as the OLYMPIA for *Rederi AB Slite* of Sweden for *Viking Line* service between Stockholm and Helsinki. In 1993 she was chartered to *P&O European Ferries* to inaugurate a new service between Portsmouth and Bilbao. During the summer period she also operates, at weekends, a round trip between Portsmouth and Cherbourg. In 1993 she was purchased by the *Irish Continental Group* and re-registered in the Bahamas. However, she is expected to remain on charter to *P&O European Ferries* until 2003.

PRIDE OF BRUGES Built as the PRIDE OF FREE ENTERPRISE for the Dover – Calais service, also operating on the Dover – Zeebrugge service during the winter. She was renamed the PRIDE OF BRUGES in 1988 and, following the delivery of the new PRIDE OF CALAIS, she was transferred all year to the Dover – Zeebrugge service. In 1992 she returned to the Dover – Calais route, but still also acts as a relief on the Dover – Zeebrugge freight service.

PRIDE OF BURGUNDY Built for the Dover – Calais service. When construction started she was due to be a sister vessel to the EUROPEAN CLEARWAY, EUROPEAN HIGHWAY and EUROPEAN PATHWAY (see Section 4) called the EUROPEAN CAUSEWAY and operate on the Zeebrugge freight route. However, it was decided that should be completed as a passenger/freight vessel (the design allowed for conversion) and she was launched as the PRIDE OF BURGUNDY. Reserve freight vessel on the Dover – Zeebrugge freight service.

PRIDE OF CALAIS Built for the Dover – Calais service.

PRIDE OF CHERBOURG Built as the VIKING VOYAGER for the Felixstowe – Zeebrugge service. In 1986 transferred to the Portsmouth – Cherbourg service. She was transferred to the French flag for the 1986 summer season but resumed British registry in the autumn of that year. She was renamed the PRIDE OF CHERBOURG in 1989. Due to be withdrawn from service in June 1994.

PRIDE OF DOVER Built for the Dover – Calais service.

PRIDE OF FLANDERS Built as the MERZARIO ESPANIA for *Stena Line AB* of Sweden and immediately chartered to *Merzario Line* for their service between Italy and Saudi Arabia. In the same year she was renamed the MERZARIO HISPANIA. In 1979 she was chartered to *European Ferries* for their RO/RO freight service between Felixstowe and Rotterdam (Europoort) and renamed the NORDIC FERRY. In 1982 she served in the Falkland Islands Task Force. In 1986 she was modified to carry 688 passengers and, with sister vessel the BALTIC FERRY (now PRIDE OF SUFFOLK), replaced the VIKING VISCOUNT (now the PRIDE OF WINCHESTER) and the VIKING VOYAGER (now the PRIDE OF CHERBOURG) on the Felixstowe – Zeebrugge service. In 1992 she was renamed the PRIDE OF FLANDERS.

PRIDE OF HAMPSHIRE Built as the VIKING VENTURER for Southampton (from 1976 Southampton/Portsmouth and 1984 Portsmouth only) – Cherbourg/Le Havre services. Extensively rebuilt in Bremerhaven in 1986 to increase vehicle capacity in a similar way to the PRIDE OF AILSA. She was renamed the PRIDE OF HAMPSHIRE in 1989. Due to transfer to the Portsmouth – Cherbourg service in June 1994.

PRIDE OF KENT Built as the SPIRIT OF FREE ENTERPRISE for the Dover – Calais service, also operating on the Dover – Zeebrugge service during the winter. She was renamed the PRIDE OF KENT in 1987. Sister vessel of the PRIDE OF BRUGES. During winter 1991/92 she was 'stretched' in Palermo, Italy to give her similar capacity to the PRIDE OF CALAIS and the PRIDE OF DOVER. Now operates Dover – Calais only.

PRIDE OF LE HAVRE Built as the VIKING VALIANT. Details otherwise as the PRIDE OF HAMPSHIRE. Due to transfer to the Portsmouth – Cherbourg service in June 1994 and also to be renamed on entry into service of the former Olau twins - See page 28.

PRIDE OF RATHLIN Built as the FREE ENTERPRISE VII for Dover – Calais and Dover – Zeebrugge services. After the delivery of new vessels in 1980 she was generally used on the Dover – Zeebrugge service. 'Stretched' in Bremerhaven in 1985/6 in a similar way to the PRIDE OF AILSA. She was renamed the PRIDE OF WALMER in 1988. In summer 1992 she was transferred to the Cairnryan – Larne route and renamed the PRIDE OF RATHLIN.

Dana Anglia (FotoFlite)

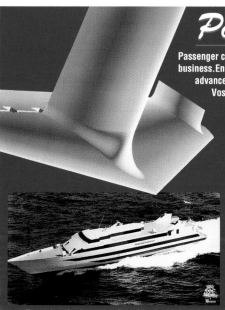

PRIDE OF SUFFOLK Built as the STENA TRANSPORTER, a RO/RO freight vessel for *Stena Line AB* of Sweden. In 1979 she was renamed the FINNROSE and chartered to *Atlanticargo* for their service between Europe and USA/Mexico. In 1980 she returned to *Stena Line* and resumed her original name. Later in 1980 she was chartered to *European Ferries* for their Felixstowe – Rotterdam (Europoort) freight only service and renamed the BALTIC FERRY. In 1982 she served in the Falkland Islands Task Force. In 1986 she was modified in the same way as the PRIDE OF FLANDERS and moved to the Felixstowe – Zeebrugge service. In 1992 she was renamed the PRIDE OF SUFFOLK.

PRIDE OF WINCHESTER Built as the VIKING VISCOUNT for the Felixstowe – Zeebrugge service. In 1986 transferred to the Portsmouth – Cherbourg service. She was renamed the PRIDE OF WINCHESTER in 1989. Due to be withdrawn from service in June 1994.

SALLY FERRIES

THE COMPANY *Sally Ferries* is the trading name of *Sally Line Limited*, a British subsidiary of *Effjohn International*, a company jointly owned by *EFFOA (Finland Steamship Company)* of Finland, The Union Bank of Finland and *Johnson Line* of Sweden. Until 1987 *Sally Line Limited* was owned by *Rederi AB Sally* of Finland. This company was named 'Sally' by its founder Algot Johansson after Åland Islands writer Sally Salminen; it became part of the *Effjohn* group in 1987.

MANAGEMENT Chairman: Michael Kingshott, Passenger Director: Linda McLeod, Freight Director: Simon Taylor.

ADDRESS Argyle Centre, York Street, RAMSGATE, Kent CT11 9DS.

TELEPHONE Administration: +44 (0)843 595566. Reservations: +44 (0)843 595522. Fax: +44 (0)843 589329. Telex: 965979.

ROUTE OPERATED Ramsgate – Dunkerque Ouest (2 hrs 30 mins; *(1,2)*; 8 per day (includes 1 freight only sailing using passenger vessels)).

VESSELS

1	SALLY SKY	*14458t	76	18.5k	1150P	323C	58L	BA2	Bremerhaven, GE	BA
2	SALLY STAR	9120t	81	19k	1800P	550C	75L	BA2	Helsinki, FI	BA

SALLY SKY Built as the GEDSER for *Gedser-Travemünde Ruten* of Denmark for their service between Gedser (Denmark) and Travemünde (Germany). In 1986 she was purchased by *Thorsviks Rederi A/S* of Norway and chartered to *Sally Ferries*, re-registered in the Bahamas, renamed the VIKING 2 and entered service on the Ramsgate – Dunkerque service. In early 1989 she was renamed the SALLY SKY and during winter 1989/90 she was 'stretched' to increase vehicle capacity.

SALLY STAR Built as the TRAVEMÜNDE for *Gedser-Travemünde Ruten* of Denmark for their service between Gedser (Denmark) and Travemünde (Germany). In 1986 the company's trading name was changed to *GT Linien* and in 1987, following the take-over by *Sea-Link AB* of Sweden, it was further changed to *GT Link*. The vessel's name was changed to the TRAVEMÜNDE LINK. In 1988 she was purchased by *Gotlandsbolaget* of Sweden, although remaining in service with *GT Link*. Later in 1988 she was chartered to *Sally Ferries* and entered service in December on the Ramsgate – Dunkerque service, replacing THE VIKING (4371t, 1974). She was renamed the SALLY STAR.

& NOW. . .
OSTEND,
RAMSGATE
& SALLY

Ferries to Ostend and Dunkerque, Jetfoils to Ostend. An ideal choice whether you are travelling for pleasure or business.

And if you travel regularly you can join our Nautical Miles scheme and collect for discounted or even free travel.

FOR MORE INFORMATION CONTACT US NOW AT:

OOSTENDE LINES, PLACE MADOU 1,
1030 BRUSSELS,
BELGIUM
TELEPHONE (2) 219 07 09
FAX (2) 219 14 94

SALLY FERRIES, ARGYLE CENTRE,
YORK STREET,
RAMSGATE, KENT CT11 9DS
TELEPHONE (0843) 595522
FAX (0843) 589329

OR SEE YOUR TRAVEL AGENT

Sally Star (FotoFlite)

Hamburg (John Hendy)

SCANDINAVIAN SEAWAYS

THE COMPANY *Scandinavian Seaways* is the trading name of the passenger division of *DFDS A/S* , a Danish private sector company. In 1981 *Tor Line* of Sweden and *Prinzen Linie* of Germany were taken over.

MANAGEMENT Managing Director UK: Ebbe Pedersen, **Passenger Director UK:** John Crummie.

ADDRESS Scandinavia House, Parkeston Quay, HARWICH, Essex CO12 4QG.

TELEPHONE Administration: +44 (0)255 243456, **Reservations:** *Harwich:* +44 (0)255 240240, *Newcastle:* +44 (0)91-293 6262. **Fax:** . 0255 244370, **Telex:** 987542.

ROUTES OPERATED All year: Harwich – Esbjerg (19 hrs 45 mins; *(1)*; 3 per week or alternate days), Harwich – Göteborg (24 hrs; *(4)*; up to 2 per week), Harwich – Hamburg (20 hrs 30 mins; *(2)*; alternate days). Summer only: Newcastle – Esbjerg (19 hrs; *(5)*; every 4 days), Newcastle – Hamburg (23 hrs 30 mins; *(5)*; every 4 days), Newcastle – Göteborg (21 hrs; *(4)*; 1 per week).

VESSELS

1	DANA ANGLIA	14400t	78	21k	1372P	470C	45L	BA	Ålborg, DK	DK
2	HAMBURG	13141t	76	22k	150P	400C	45L	BA	Rendsburg, GE	BA
3	PRINCE OF SCANDINAVIA	15794t	75	23k	1450P	420C	70T	AS	Lübeck, GE	DK
4	PRINCESS OF SCANDINAVIA	15794t	76	23k	1450P	420C	70T	AS	Lübeck, GE	DK
5	WINSTON CHURCHILL	8658t	67	20k	840P	180C	18L	BA	Genova, IT	DK

DANA ANGLIA Built for *DFDS* and used on the Harwich – Esbjerg service.

HAMBURG Built as the KRONPRINS HARALD for *Jahre Line* of Norway and used on their service between Oslo and Kiel (Germany). Acquired by *DFDS* in 1987, renamed the HAMBURG, re-registered in the Bahamas and replaced the PRINS HAMLET (5830t, 1973) on the Harwich – Hamburg service.

PRINCE OF SCANDINAVIA Built as the TOR BRITANNIA for *Tor Line* of Sweden for their Amsterdam – Göteborg and Felixstowe – Göteborg services. She was acquired by *DFDS* in 1981 and subsequently re-registered in Denmark. Since winter 1983/4 she has also operated on the Harwich – Esbjerg service with the DANA ANGLIA. She has also operated Newcastle – Esbjerg and Amsterdam – Göteborg. During winter 1989/90 she was used as an accommodation ship for refugees in Malmö. In 1991 renamed the PRINCE OF SCANDINAVIA following a major refurbishment. In summer 1994 she is due to operate on the Ijmuiden (Netherlands) – Göteborg (Sweden) and Ijmuiden – Kristiansand (Norway) service and not serve the UK. However, she is included as she may serve the UK during the winter and during future summers.

PRINCESS OF SCANDINAVIA Built as the TOR SCANDINAVIA for *Tor Line* of Sweden for their Amsterdam – Göteborg and Felixstowe – Göteborg services. In 1979 she was used on a world trade cruise and was temporarily renamed the HOLLAND EXPO. Similar exercises were undertaken in 1980, 1982 and 1984, but on these occasions the name was the WORLD WIDE EXPO. She was acquired by *DFDS* in 1981 and subsequently re-registered in Denmark. She has also operated on the Harwich – Esbjerg service with the DANA ANGLIA although this arrangement has now ceased. Since summer 1989 she has also operated Newcastle – Esbjerg and Amsterdam – Göteborg services. In 1991 renamed the PRINCESS OF SCANDINAVIA following a major refurbishment. During summer 1994 she will operate on the Harwich – Göteborg and Newcastle – Göteborg services.

WINSTON CHURCHILL Built for *DFDS* for the Harwich – Esbjerg service. When DANA ANGLIA was introduced in 1978 she inaugurated a new twice weekly service from Newcastle to Göteborg, jointly with *Tor Line* until *Tor Line* was taken over by *DFDS* in 1981. In 1981 she took over the seasonal Newcastle – Esbjerg – Tórshavn service from the ENGLAND (8117t, 1964). In summer 1984 she operated a service between København and Tórshavn and did not visit Britain but in 1985 she resumed her previous role. Since 1987 she also operated cruises in the spring and autumn periods (Baltic and North Cape). During winter 1989/90 she was used as an accommodation ship for refugees in Malmö. In 1993 she inaugurated a new Newcastle – Hamburg service, alternating with her Newcastle – Esbjerg service. The Esbjerg – Tórshavn service ceased at the end of the 1992 summer season.

Scandinavian Seaways also operate two vessels between København and Oslo. They are KING OF SCANDINAVIA (20581t, 1975 (ex DANA GLORIA 1988, ex WELLAMO 1981)) and QUEEN OF SCANDINAVIA (25905t, 1981 (ex FINLANDIA 1990)).

SEALINK – SNAT

THE COMPANY *SNAT (Société Nouvelle Armement Transmanche)* is a French company. It is jointly owned by *Société National des Chemins de fer Français* (French Railways), *Compagnie Générale Maritime Français* (French National Shipping Company) and *Stena Sealink Ltd.* It was established in 1990 to take over the services of *SNCF Armement Naval*, a wholly owned division of SNCF. At the same time a similarly constituted body called *Société Proprietaire Navires (SPN)* was established to take over ownership of the vessels.

MANAGEMENT **Président du Directoire:** M Bonnet, **Directeur Sealink Calais:** M Jachet.

ADDRESS 3 rue Ambrose Paré, 75475, PARIS Cedex 10, France.

TELEPHONE **Administration:** +33 1 49 95 58 98. **Reservations:** *France:* +33 21 96 70 70, *UK* +44 (0)233 647047 *(Stena Sealink Line)* **Fax:** . +33 1 48 74 62 37. **Telex:** 280549.

ROUTE OPERATED Calais – Dover (1 hr 30 mins; *(1,2)*; up to 25 per day (joint with *Stena Sealink Line*).

VESSELS

1	COTE D'AZUR	8862t	81	18k	1600P	330C	54T	BA2	Le Havre, FR	FR
2	FIESTA	*25122t	80	19.5k	1800P	600C	150T	BA2	Malmö, SW	FR

COTE D'AZUR Built for *SNCF* for Dover – Calais service. Also operated Boulogne – Dover in 1985.

FIESTA Built as the ARIADNE for *Rederi AB Nordö* of Sweden. Renamed SOCA before entering service on *UMEF* freight services (but with capacity for 175 drivers) in the Mediterranean. In 1981 she was sold to *SO Mejdunaroden Automobilen Transport (SOMAT)* of Bulgaria and renamed the TRAPEZITZA. She operated on *Medlink* services between Bulgaria and the Middle East. In 1988 she was acquired by *Sealink*, re-registered in the Bahamas and in 1989 renamed the FANTASIA. Later in 1989 she was modified in Bremerhaven, renamed the CHANNEL SEAWAY and, in May, she inaugurated a new freight only service between Dover (Eastern Docks) and Calais. During winter 1989/90 she was modified in Bremerhaven to convert her for passenger service. In spring 1990 she was renamed the FIESTA, transferred to *SNAT*, re-registered in France and replaced the CHAMPS ELYSEES (see the STENA PARISIEN, *Stena Sealink Line*) on the Dover – Calais service.

The Floor
will make quite an impression.
The passengers won't.

Works of art you can walk on.

Lightweight practical solutions for marine installations worldwide. Amtico International, Coventry, England.
Telephone + (44) 203 861 501. Fax + (44) 203 861558. Contact Simon Mercer

Stena Felicity (Miles Cowsill)

Stena Fantasia and The Princess Margaret (FotoFlite)

STENA LINE

THE COMPANY *Stena Line* is the trading name of *Stena Line bv* of The Netherlands, a wholly owned subsidiary of *Stena Line AB* of Sweden. *Stena Line* acquired the previous operator of this route, the Dutch *Stoomvaart Maatschappij Zeeland (Zeeland Steamship Company)* (which had since the start of 1989 traded as *Crown Line*) in summer 1989. Joint operation of the route with *Sealink* ceased in 1990, although *Stena Sealink Line* continue to market the service in the UK and Irish Republic.

MANAGEMENT **Managing Director:** Bo Severed, **Marketing and Sales Director:** Harry Betist.

ADDRESS PO Box 2, 3150 AA, Hoek van Holland.

TELEPHONE **Administration:** +31 (0)1747 89333. **Reservations:** +31 (0)1747 84140, **Fax:** +31 (0)1747 87047. **Telex:** 31272.

ROUTE OPERATED Hoek van Holland (Netherlands) – Harwich (6 hrs 30 mins (day), 8 hrs 30 mins (night); *(1,2,3)*; 3 per day).

VESSELS

1	KONINGIN BEATRIX	*31189t	86	21k	2100P	200C	96L	BA	Krimpen, NL	NL
2	STENA EUROPE	17423t	81	20.4k	2076P	500C	78T	BA2	Göteborg, SW	SW
3	STENA SEATRADER	6962t	73	17.5k	221P	–	170T	A2	Nakskov, DK	NL

KONINGIN BEATRIX Built for *Stoomvaart Maatschappij Zeeland* for the Hoek van Holland – Harwich service.

STENA EUROPE Built as KRONPRINSESSAN VICTORIA for *Göteborg – Frederikshavnlinjen* of Sweden (trading as *Sessan Line*) for their Göteborg – Frederikshavn service. Shortly after delivery, the company was taken over by *Stena Line* and services were marketed as *Stena – Sessan Line* for a period. In 1982 she was converted to an overnight ferry by the conversion of one vehicle deck to two additional decks of cabins and she was switched to the Göteborg – Kiel route (with, during the summer, daytime runs from Göteborg to Frederikshavn and Kiel to Korsør (Denmark)). In 1989 she was transferred to the Oslo – Frederikshavn route and renamed the STENA SAGA. In 1994, transferred to *Stena Line bv*, renamed the STENA EUROPE and replaced the STENA BRITANNICA, which had been transferred to *Stena Line AB* to operate between Oslo and Frederikshavn and renamed the STENA SAGA.

STENA SEATRADER Built as the SVEALAND for *Lion Ferry AB* of Sweden and chartered to *Statens Järnvägar (Swedish State Railways)* for the train ferry service between Ystad (Sweden) and Sassnitz (East Germany). The charter ceased in 1980 and in 1982 she was sold to *Rederi AB Nordö* of Sweden. She was stretched by 33.7 metres, renamed the SVEALAND AV MALMÖ and used on their lorry/rail wagon service between Malmö and Travemünde. In 1986 she was rebuilt with a higher superstructure and in 1987 she was renamed the SVEA LINK, the service being renamed *Nordö Link*. In 1990 she was sold to *Stena Line*, renamed the STENA SEATRADER and introduced onto the Hoek van Holland – Harwich service. From 1993 she has also, during the summer, carried cars towing caravans, motor caravans and their passengers – hence her inclusion in this section of the book.

STENA SEALINK LINE

THE COMPANY *Stena Sealink Line* is the trading name of *Stena Sealink Ltd*, a British private sector company. It was purchased (as *Sealink UK Ltd*) from the state owned *British Railways Board* in summer 1984 by *British Ferries Ltd*, a wholly owned subsidiary of *Sea Containers* of Bermuda. In 1990 most services and vessels were purchased from *Sea Containers* by *Stena Line AB* of Sweden – although the Isle of Wight vessels and services were excluded. In late 1990 the trading name was changed to *Sealink Stena Line* and in 1993 changed to *Stena Sealink Line*. *Stena Line* is named after its founder, Sten A Olsson.

MANAGEMENT Managing Director: W Gareth Cooper, **Marketing Director:** John Govett.

ADDRESS Charter House, Park Street, ASHFORD, Kent TN24 8EX.

TELEPHONE Administration: +44 (0)233 647022, **Reservations:** +44 (0)233 647047.

ROUTES OPERATED Stranraer – Larne (2 hrs 20 mins; *(1,2,7)*; 9 per day), Holyhead – Dun Laoghaire (3 hrs 30 mins; *(3,8)*; 4 per day), Fishguard – Rosslare (3 hrs 30 mins; *(6)*; 2 per day), Newhaven – Dieppe (4 hrs; *(10,12)*; 4 per day), Southampton – Cherbourg (5 hrs; *(11)*; 1 or 2 per day), Dover – Calais (1 hr 30 mins; *(4,5,9)*; up to 25 per day (joint with *Sealink SNAT*)).

VESSELS

1	STENA ANTRIM	7399t	81	19.5k	1350P	310C	62T	BA2	Belfast, GB	GB
2	STENA CALEDONIA	7196t	81	19.5k	1000P	310C	62T	BA2	Belfast, GB	GB
3	STENA CAMBRIA	7405t	80	19.5k	1350P	310C	62T	BA2	Belfast, GB	GB
4	STENA CHALLENGER	*18523t	90	18k	500P	–	100L	BA2	Fosen, NO	GB
5	STENA FANTASIA	*25243t	80	19.5k	1800P	600C	150T	BA2	Malmö, SW	BA
6	STENA FELICITY	15001t	80	21k	1800P	515C	45L	BAS	Landskrona, SW	SW
7	STENA GALLOWAY	6630t	80	19.0k	1000P	296C	62T	BA2	Belfast, GB	GB
8	STENA HIBERNIA	7836t	77	19.5k	1700P	310C	28T	BA	Ålborg, DK	GB
9	STENA INVICTA	*19763t	85	19.3k	2000P	400C	50T	BA2	Nakskov, DK	GB
10	STENA LONDONER	6737t	74	22k	1800P	425C	51L	BA2	Trogir, YU	BA
11	STENA NORMANDY	17043t	82	20.4k	2100P	480C	52L	BA2	Göteborg, SW	BA
12	STENA PARISIEN	*15093t	84	18k	1800P	330C	54T	BA2	Nantes, FR	FR

STENA ANTRIM Built as the ST CHRISTOPHER for *Sealink* for the Dover – Calais service. Before taking up duty on that route she substituted on the Fishguard – Rosslare service. During spring 1983 she was modified to increase passenger capacity from 1000 (later 1200) to 1400 and improve passenger facilities. In 1991 she was renamed the STENA ANTRIM and later transferred to the Stranraer – Larne route.

STENA CALEDONIA Built as the ST DAVID for *Sealink* for Holyhead – Dun Laoghaire and Fishguard – Rosslare services. It was originally planned that she would replace the chartered STENA NORMANDICA (5607t, 1975 – the vessel which subsequently became the ST BRENDAN) but it was subsequently decided that an additional large vessel (which could deputise for the ST COLUMBA and the STENA NORMANDICA) was required for the Irish Sea routes. Until 1985 her normal use was, therefore, to substitute for other Irish Sea vessels as necessary (including the Stranraer – Larne route) and also to operate additional summer services on the Holyhead – Dun Laoghaire route. During the spring of 1983 she operated on the Dover – Calais service while the ST CHRISTOPHER (now the STENA ANTRIM) was being modified. From March 1985 she operated between Dover and Oostende, a service which ceased in December 1985 with the decision of *RMT* to become part of the *Townsend Thoresen* network. During the early part of 1986 she operated between Dover and Calais and then moved to the Stranraer – Larne route where she has become a regular vessel. In 1991 she was renamed the STENA CALEDONIA.

Cote d'Azur (John Hendy)

Koningin Beatrix (Stena Line)

STENA CAMBRIA Built for *Sealink* as the ST ANSELM for the Dover – Calais service. During winter 1982/3 she was modified to increase passenger capacity from 1200 to 1400 and improve passenger facilities. In February 1990 she replaced the HORSA (5496t, 1972) on the Folkestone – Boulogne service. In 1991 she was moved to the Irish sea to operate between Holyhead and Dun Laoghaire. In 1990 she was renamed the STENA CAMBRIA.

STENA CHALLENGER Built for *Stena Rederi AB* of Sweden and chartered to *Stena Sealink Line* for Dover – Calais and Dover – Dunkerque freight services. Her hull was constructed and launched in Landskrona, Sweden and towed to Norway for fitting out. Although primarily a freight vessel, her passenger capacity of 500 allows her to be used on a relief basis at other times. In 1992 she was switched to the Dover – Dunkerque freight services, operating with NORD PAS-DE-CALAIS. In summer 1994 she is due to operate passenger services between Dover and Calais.

STENA FANTASIA Built as the SCANDINAVIA for *Rederi AB Nordö* of Sweden. After service in the Mediterranean for *UMEF*, she was, in 1981, sold to *SOMAT* of Bulgaria, renamed the TZAREVETZ and used on *Medlink* services between Bulgaria and the Middle East and later on other routes. In 1986 she was chartered to *Callitzis* of Greece for a service between Italy and Greece. In 1988 she was sold to *Sealink*, re-registered in the Bahamas and renamed the FIESTA. She was then chartered to *OT Africa Line*. During autumn 1989 she was modified in Bremerhaven to convert her for passenger use and in March 1990 she was renamed the FANTASIA and replaced the ST ANSELM on the Dover – Calais service. Later in 1990 she was renamed the STENA FANTASIA.

STENA FELICITY Built as the VISBY for *Gotlandsbolaget* of Sweden for their services between the island of Gotland and the Swedish mainland. In 1987, the franchise to operate these services was lost by the company and awarded to *Nordström & Thulin* of Sweden. A subsidiary called *Gotlandslinjen* was formed to operate the service. The VISBY was chartered to this company and managed by *Johnson Line*, remaining owned by *Gotlandsbolaget*. In early 1990 she was chartered to *Sealink* and renamed the FELICITY. After modifications at Tilbury, she was, in March 1990, introduced onto the Fishguard – Rosslare route. In 1991 she was renamed the STENA FELICITY.

STENA GALLOWAY Built as the GALLOWAY PRINCESS for *Sealink* for the Stranraer – Larne service. In 1990 renamed the STENA GALLOWAY.

STENA HIBERNIA Built as the ST COLUMBA for *Sealink* for the Holyhead – Dun Laoghaire service to replace separate classic and car ferry services with a single multi-purpose vessel, performing two round trips per day. She has also been used on the Fishguard – Rosslare service. During winter 1982/3 she was modified to change her from a two-class to a single class vessel. She was further extensively rebuilt over winter 1990/91 and was renamed the STENA HIBERNIA.

STENA INVICTA Built as the PEDER PAARS for *DSB (Danish State Railways)* for their service between Kalundborg (Sealand) and Århus (Jutland). In 1990 purchased by *Stena Line AB* of Sweden for delivery in 1991. In 1991 renamed the STENA INVICTA and entered service on the Dover – Calais service, replacing the STENA CAMBRIA. She is sister vessel of *B&I Line's* ISLE OF INNISFREE.

STENA LONDONER Built as the STENA DANICA for *Stena Line AB* of Sweden for their Göteborg – Frederikshavn service. In 1982, in anticipation of the delivery of a new STENA DANICA, being built in France, she was renamed the STENA NORDICA. In June 1983 she was taken by *RMT* on a three year charter, introduced onto *RMT's* Oostende – Dover service and re-registered in Belgium. In March 1984 she was renamed the STENA NAUTICA. The charter ended in June 1986 when the PRINS ALBERT re-entered service; she returned to *Stena Line* and was re-registered in The Bahamas. In 1987 she was sold to *SNCF*, re-registered in France, renamed the VERSAILLES and introduced onto the Dieppe – Newhaven service. Chartered to *Stena Sealink Line* in May 1992, re-registered in The Bahamas and renamed the STENA LONDONER.

STENA NORMANDY One of two vessels ordered by *Göteborg – Frederikshavnlinjen* of Sweden (trading as *Sessan Line*) before the take over of their operations by *Stena Line AB* in 1981. Both were designed for the Göteborg – Frederikshavn route (a journey of about three hours). However, *Stena Line* decided in 1982 to switch the first vessel, the KRONPRINSESSAN VICTORIA (now the STENA EUROPE of *Stena Line bv*), to their Göteborg – Kiel (Germany) route since their own new tonnage for this route, being built in Poland, had been substantially delayed. She was modified to make her more suitable for this overnight route. Work on the second vessel – provisionally called the DROTTNING SILVIA – was suspended for a time but she was eventually delivered, as designed, in late 1982 and introduced onto the Göteborg – Frederikshavn route on a temporary basis pending delivery of new *Stena Line* ordered vessels. She was named the PRINSESSAN BIRGITTA, the existing ex *Sessan Line* vessel of the same name being renamed the STENA SCANDINAVICA (see the VENUS, *Color Line*). In early 1983 she was substantially modified in a similar way to her sister. In June 1983 she was renamed the ST NICHOLAS, re-registered in Great Britain and entered service on five year charter to *Sealink UK* on the Harwich – Hoek van Holland route. In 1988 she was purchased and re-registered in The Bahamas. In 1989 she was sold to *Gotlandsbolaget* of Sweden and then chartered back for a five year period. In 1991 she was renamed the STENA NORMANDY and inaugurated a new service between Southampton and Cherbourg.

STENA PARISIEN Built for *SNCF* as the CHAMPS ELYSEES to operate Calais – Dover and Boulogne – Dover services, later operating Calais – Dover only. In 1990 transferred to the Dieppe – Newhaven service. Chartered to *Stena Sealink Line* in June 1992, and renamed the STENA PARISIEN.

STRANDFARASKIP LANDSINS

THE COMPANY *Strandfaraskip Landsins* is the Faroe Islands state shipping company. It ceased services to the UK when *Smyril Line* was established in 1983 but re-established sailings during summer 1989.

MANAGEMENT Managing Director: Thomas Magnussen, Marketing Manager: Ms Unn A Lad.

ADDRESS Postboks 88, FR-110, Tórshavn, FAROE ISLANDS.

TELEPHONE Administration: +298 14550, Reservations: *Faroe Islands:* +298 14550, *UK:* +44 (0)224 572615 *(P&O Scottish Ferries)*, Fax: +298 16000, Telex: 81295.

ROUTE OPERATED Tórshavn (Faroes) – Aberdeen (21 hrs; *(1)*; 1 per week) - operated by *Smyril Line*

VESSEL

SMYRIL	2430t	69	18k	500P	120C	16L	BA	Ålborg, DK	FA

SMYRIL Built as the MORTEN MOLS for *Mols Linien A/S* of Denmark (a subsidiary of *DFDS*) for their internal Danish service between Ebeltoft (Jutland) and Sjaellands Odde (Sealand). She was purchased by *Strandfaraskip Landsins* in 1975 to inaugurate RO/RO services to and from the Faroe islands and the UK, Denmark and Norway and renamed the SMYRIL. Used only on inter-island services between 1983 and 1989. In 1989 international services were resumed. She was chartered out in 1991 and the service was operated by sister vessel the TEISTIN (4269t, 1969 (ex MIKKEL MOLS 1975)). She resumed the service in March 1992.

Superferry (Miles Cowsill)

Barfleur (Brittany Ferries)

SWANSEA CORK FERRIES

THE COMPANY *Swansea Cork Ferries* is a company established in 1987 to re-open the Swansea – Cork service abandoned by *B&I Line* in 1979. It was jointly owned by West Glamorgan County Council, Cork Corporation, Cork County Council and Kerry County Council. The service did not operate in 1989 but resumed in 1990. It 1993 it was acquired by *Strintzis Line* of Greece.

MANAGEMENT Managing Director: Thomas Hunter McGowan, **Marketing Manager:** Desmond Donnelly.

ADDRESS 52 South Mall, CORK, Republic of Ireland.

TELEPHONE Administration: +353 (0)21 276000, **Reservations:** *IR:* +353 (0)21 271166, *UK:* +44 (0)792 456116, **Fax:** *IR:* +353 (0)21 275814, *UK:* +44 (0)792 644356.

ROUTE OPERATED Swansea – Cork (10 hrs; *(1)*; 1 per day or alternate days, according to season).

VESSEL

SUPERFERRY	7454t	72	21.8k	1365P	550C	80T	BA	Hashihama, JA	GR

SUPERFERRY Built as the CASSIOPEIA for *Ocean Ferry KK* of Japan. In 1976 the company became *Ocean Tokyu Ferry KK* and she was renamed the IZU NO 3. She was used on the service between Tokyo (Honshu) – Tokushima (Shikoko) – Kokura (Kyshu). In 1991 she was sold to *Strintzis Line* and briefly renamed the IONIAN STAR. Following major rebuilding, she was renamed the SUPERFERRY and used on their services between Greece and Italy. In 1993 transferred to *Swansea Cork Ferries*.

TRUCKLINE FERRIES

THE COMPANY *Truckline Ferries* is *Brittany Ferries'* freight division. However, it also operates passenger services.

MANAGEMENT As *Brittany Ferries*.

TELEPHONE Administration: +44 (0)202 667388. **Reservations:** +44 (0)202 666466.

ROUTE OPERATED Cherbourg – Poole (4 hrs 15 mins; *(1)*; 2 per day).

VESSEL

BARFLEUR	*20500t	92	19k	1173P	550C	125T	BA	Helsinki, FI	FR

BARFLEUR Built for *Truckline Ferries* for their Cherbourg – Poole service to replace two passenger vessels – the CORBIERE (4371t, 1970) and the TREGASTEL (see the ST CLAIR, *P&O Scottish Ferries*) – and to inaugurate a year round passenger service.

SECTION 2 – FAST FERRIES

CONDOR

THE COMPANY, MANAGEMENT, ADDRESS AND TELEPHONE See Section 1.

VESSEL

CONDOR 10		*3241t	93	37k	580P	80C	–	BA	Hobart, AL	SI

CONDOR 10 Built for *Condor*.

Condor also operates high speed passenger only services using: CONDOR 7 (174t, 1976, 180 passengers, hydrofoil), CONDOR 8 (387t, 1988, 300 passengers, catamaran). **Routes operated:** St Malo – Channel Islands and internal services between Jersey, Guernsey and Sark.

EMERAUDE LINES

THE COMPANY, MANAGEMENT, ADDRESS & TELEPHONE: See section 1.

ROUTES OPERATED St Malo – St Helier (Jersey) (1 hr 20 mins; *(1)*; up to 3 per day), St Malo – St Peter Port (Guernsey) (1 hr 45 mins; *(1)*; 1 per day). Service starts 15 May 1994.

VESSEL

EMERAUDE		–	94	32k	400P	45C	–	BA	St Malo, FR	FR

EMERAUDE Built for *Emeraude Ferries*. Unlike most other fast ferries she is of monohull construction.

The company also operates catamaran ferries TRIDENT 3 (251t, 1982), TRIDENT 4 (248t, 1981), TRIDENT 5 (251t, 1974), TRIDENT 6 (287t, 1981), TRIDENT 7 (234t,1979) and PEGASUS (on charter) (249t, 1976) on various routes from France to the Channel Islands. No cars are conveyed.

HOVERSPEED

THE COMPANY *Hoverspeed* is a British private sector company. It was formed in October 1981 by the merger of *Seaspeed*, a wholly owned subsidiary of the British Railways Board, operating between Dover and Calais and Dover and Boulogne and *Hoverlloyd*, a subsidiary of *Broström AB* of Sweden, operating between Ramsgate (Pegwell Bay) and Calais. The Ramsgate – Calais service ceased after summer 1982. In early 1984 the Company was sold by its joint owners to a management consortium. In 1986 the company was acquired by *Sea Containers*. It was retained by *Sea Containers* in 1990 following the sale of most of *Sealink British Ferries* to *Stena Line* of Sweden. Hovercraft services were supplemented by wave piercing catamarans (SeaCats) in 1991 and during winter 1991/92 no hovercraft services were operated. However, since summer 1992, an all year hovercraft service has run between Dover Hoverport and Calais.

Emeraulde (Emeraude Line)

Condor 10 (FotoFlite)

MANAGEMENT Managing Director: Geoffrey Ede, **Marketing Manager:** John Smith.

ADDRESS International Hoverport, Marine Parade, DOVER, Kent CT17 9TG.

TELEPHONE Administration: +44 (0)304 240101, **Reservations:** +44 (0)304 240241. **Fax:** +44 (0)304 240088.

ROUTES OPERATED SeaCats: Dover – Calais (50 mins; *(2,3)*; up to 8 per day), Folkestone – Boulogne (55 mins; *(2,3)*; up to 6 per day), Stranraer – Belfast (1 hrs 30 mins; *(1,4)*; up to 6 per day). Hovercraft: Dover – Calais (35 mins; *(5,6)*; up to 12 per day).

VESSELS

1	HOVERSPEED GREAT BRITAIN	*3003t	90	37k	432P	80C	–	BA	Hobart, AL	BA
2	SEACAT BOULOGNE	*3003t	91	37k	400P	80C	–	BA	Hobart, AL	BA
3	SEACAT CALAIS	*3012t	90	35k	350P	80C	.	BA	Hobart, AL	BA
4	SEACAT SCOTLAND	*3003t	91	37k	432P	80C	–	BA	Hobart, AL	BA
5	THE PRINCESS ANNE	–	69	60k	390P	55C	–	BA	Cowes, GB	GB
6	THE PRINCESS MARGARET	–	68	60k	390P	55C	–	BA	Cowes, GB	GB

HOVERSPEED GREAT BRITAIN Launched as the CHRISTOPHER COLUMBUS but renamed before entering service. Built for Hoverspeed to inaugurate a new car and passenger service between Portsmouth and Cherbourg. This service was suspended in early 1991 and later that year she was, after modification, switched to a new service between Dover (Eastern Docks) and Boulogne/Calais, replacing hovercraft. In 1992 operated on Channel routes. During winter 1992/3 she was chartered to *Ferry Lineas* of Argentina, operating between Buenos Aires (Argentina) and Montevideo (Uruguay). Now operates mainly between Stranraer and Belfast to provide a two vessel service with the SEACAT SCOTLAND.

SEACAT BOULOGNE Built as HOVERSPEED FRANCE, the second SeaCat. She inaugurated Dover – Calais/Boulogne service in 1991. Now operates on all three Channel routes (see above). In 1992 she was chartered to *Sardinia Express* and did not operate on the Channel. This charter was terminated at the end of 1992 and in 1993 she was renamed the SEACAT BOULOGNE. She operates on the Dover – Calais and Folkestone – Boulogne services

SEACAT CALAIS Built as SEACAT TASMANIA for *Tasmanian Ferry Services* of Australia to operate between George Town (Tasmania) and Port Welshpool (Victoria). In 1992 chartered to *Hoverspeed* to operate Dover – Calais and Folkestone – Boulogne services. Returned to Australia after the 1992 summer season but returned to Britain in summer 1993 to operate Dover – Calais and Folkestone – Boulogne services during the summer. She was repainted into *Hoverspeed* livery and renamed the SEACAT CALAIS. Due to be chartered for five years in 1994.

SEACAT SCOTLAND Fifth SeaCat to be built, used on Stranraer – Belfast service.

THE PRINCESS ANNE Hovercraft built for *Seaspeed.* BHC SRN4 type. Built to Mark I specification. In 1978 stretched to Mark III specification.

THE PRINCESS MARGARET Hovercraft built for *Seaspeed.* BHC SRN4 type. Built to Mark I specification.[*] In 1979 stretched to Mark III specification.

Note: The fourth SeaCat to be built for the *Sea Containers Group*, christened after launching in 1991 as the HOVERSPEED BELGIUM but renamed the HOVERSPEED BOULOGNE before entering service in 1992, is now in service between Göteborg (Sweden) and Frederikshavn (Denmark) and has been renamed the SEACATAMARAN DANMARK.

STENA SEALINK LINE

THE COMPANY, MANAGEMENT AND TELEPHONE: See section 1.

ROUTE OPERATED Holyhead – Dun Laoghaire (1 hr 50 mins; *(1)*; up to 4 per day).

1	STENA SEA LYNX	*3003t	93	40k	450P	90C	–	BA	Hobart, AL		BA

STENA SEA LYNX Second of two vessels ordered for *Condor*. Whilst the first became the CONDOR 10, the option on the second (intended to be the CONDOR 11) was cancelled and she was instead chartered to *Stena Sealink Line* and, in July 1993, she started a new high speed service between Holyhead and Dun Laoghaire.

Under construction:

2	NEWBUILDING 1	–	95	40k	1500P	375C	50L	BA	Rauma, FI	–
3	NEWBUILDING 2	–	96	40k	1500P	375C	50L	BA	Rauma, FI	–

NEWBUILDING 1 Under construction for *Stena Line*. It is the current intention that she should operate on the Holyhead – Dun Laoghaire service.

NEWBUILDING 2 Under construction for *Stena Line*. The deployment of this vessel has yet to be decided and it may be that she will not serve with *Stena Sealink Line*.

Newbuilding - HSS Craft (Stena Sealink Line)

SECTION 3 – DOMESTIC SERVICES – ISLAND AND ESTUARIAL

BERE ISLAND FERRIES

THE COMPANY *Bere Island Ferries Ltd* is an Irish Republic private sector company.

MANAGEMENT Operator: C Harrington.

ADDRESS Ferry House, West End, Bere Island, County Cork, Republic of Ireland.

TELEPHONE Administration: +353 (0)27 75009. **Reservations:** Not applicable.

ROUTE OPERATED Castletownbere (County Cork) – Bere Island (10 mins; *(1)*; up to 10 per day).

VESSEL

1	MISNEACH		30t	78	7k	80P	4C	–	B	New Ross, IR	IR

MISNEACH Built for *Maoin-na-Farraige* of the Irish Republic and used on their Burtonpoint – Arranmore service. In 1992 sold to *Bere Island Ferries*. In 1993 inaugurated a car ferry service between Castletownbere and Bere Island.

CALEDONIAN MACBRAYNE

THE COMPANY *Caledonian MacBrayne* is a British state owned company, the responsibility of the Secretary of State for Scotland. Until 1st April 1990 it was part of the state owned *Scottish Transport Group* (formed in 1969). *Caledonian MacBrayne* was formed in 1973 by the merger of the *Caledonian Steam Packet Company* (which had been formed in 1889) and *David MacBrayne Ltd* (whose origins go back to 1851).

MANAGEMENT Managing Director: C S Paterson CBE, **Marketing Manager:** W J H Bowie.

ADDRESS The Ferry Terminal, GOUROCK PA19 1QP.

TELEPHONE Administration: +44 (0)475 650100, **Reservations:** +44 (0)475 650000, **Fax:** +44 (0)475 637607, **Telex:** 779318.

ROUTES OPERATED Ardrossan – Brodick (Arran) (55 mins; *(2)*; up to 6 per day), Ardrossan – Douglas (Isle of Man) (in association with *Isle of Man Steam Packet*) (8 hrs; *(5)*; 1 per week), Lochranza – Claonaig (Arran) (30 mins; *(22)*; up to 10 per day), Largs – Cumbrae Slip (Cumbrae) (10 mins; *(18,21)*; every 30 or 15 mins), Wemyss Bay – Rothesay (Bute) (30 mins; *(13,14,26,29)*; up to 22 per day), Rothesay (Bute) – Brodick (Arran) (1 hr 30 mins; *(26)*; 2 per week), Colintraive – Rhubodach (Bute) (5 mins; *(20)*; frequent service), Tarbert (Loch Fyne) – Portavadie (20 mins; *(28)*; up to 11 per day), Gourock – Dunoon (20 mins; *(13,14,29)*; hourly service with extras at peaks), Gourock – Kilcreggan (10 mins; *(13,14,29)*; charter service for RNAD workers plus 2 public crossings – no cars conveyed), Kennacraig – Port Ellen (Islay) (2 hrs 15 mins; *(10)*; 1 or 2 per day), Kennacraig – Port Askaig (Islay) (2 hrs; *(10)*; 1 or 2 per day), Oban – Colonsay – Port Askaig (3 hrs 35 mins; *(10)*; 1 per week), Tayinloan – Gigha (20 mins; *(19)*; hourly with some gaps), Oban – Lismore (50 mins; *(7)*; up to 4 per day), Oban – Colonsay (2 hrs 10 mins; *(10,12)*; 3 per week), Oban – Craignure (Mull) (40 mins; *(12)*; two hourly), Oban – Coll (2 hrs 45 mins (direct), 4 hrs 50 mins (via Tiree); *(24)*; up to 5 per

Caledonian Isles (Caledonian MacBrayne)

Loch Riddon (Lawrence MacDuff)

week), Oban – Tiree (3 hrs 30 mins (direct), 4 hrs 15 mins (via Coll); *(24)*; up to 5 per week), Oban – Castlebay (Barra) (5 hrs (direct); *(24)*; 4 per week), Oban – Lochboisdale (South Uist) (5 hrs (direct), 7hrs (via Barra); *(24)*; 5 per week), Lochaline – Fishnish (Mull) (15 mins; *(11)*; up to 16 per day), Fionnphort (Mull) – Iona (5 mins; *(15)*; frequent) (passengers only; residents' private cars and service vehicles conveyed by special arrangement), Tobermory (Mull) – Kilchoan (35 mins; *(1,6)*; up to 11 per day), Mallaig – Armadale (Skye)(cars and passengers – summer only) (30 mins; *(9)*; up to 7 per day), Mallaig – Armadale (Skye)(passenger only October – Easter) (30 mins; *(23)*; up to 2 per day), Mallaig – Eigg – Muck – Rum – Canna – Mallaig (passenger only) (round trip 7 hrs (all islands); *(23)*; at least 1 sailing per day – most islands visited daily), Mallaig – Kyle of Lochalsh (passenger only) (2 hrs; *(23)*; 1 per week), Mallaig – Lochboisdale (South Uist) (3 hrs 30 mins; *(9)*; 2 per week), Mallaig – Castlebay (Barra) (via Lochboisdale) (5 hrs 30 mins; *(9)*; 2 per week), Kyle of Lochalsh – Kyleakin (Skye) (5 mins; *(16,17)*; frequent), Sconser (Skye) – Raasay (15 mins; *(27)*; up to 10 per day), Uig (Skye) – Tarbert (Harris) (1 hr 45 mins; *(8)*; 1 or 2 per day), Uig (Skye) – Lochmaddy (North Uist) (1 hr 45 mins; *(8)*; 1 or 2 per day), Tarbert – Lochmaddy (1 hr 45 mins; *(8)*; 3 direct per week (all other sailings via Uig)), Kyles Scalpay (Harris) – Scalpay (10 mins; *(4)*; up to 13 per day), Ullapool – Stornoway (Lewis) (3 hrs 30 mins; *(30)*; up to 3 per day).

Clyde Cruising In addition to normal car and passenger service, the following cruises are operated in the Clyde; parts of these cruises are normal car/passenger services: Gourock – Dunoon – Wemyss Bay – Rothesay – Tighnabruaich ((*13,14,29*); 2 per week), Gourock – Dunoon – Largs – Rothesay – Tarbert (Loch Fyne) ((*13,14,29*); 1 per week), Gourock – Dunoon – Rothesay – Brodick ((*13,14,26,29*); 2 per week).

VESSELS

1	BRUERNISH	69t	73	8k	164P	6C	–	B	Port Glasgow, GB	GB
2	CALEDONIAN ISLES	*5221t	93	15k	1000P	120C	–	BA	Lowestoft, GB	GB
4	CANNA	69t	73	8k	164P	6C	–	B	Port Glasgow, GB	GB
5	CLAYMORE	1631t	78	15.5k	500P	50C	–	AS	Leith, GB	GB
6	COLL	69t	74	8k	154P	6C	–	B	Port Glasgow, GB	GB
7	EIGG	69t	75	8k	164P	6C	–	B	Port Glasgow, GB	GB
8	HEBRIDEAN ISLES	*3040t	85	15k	510P	68C	10L	BAS	Selby, GB	GB
9	IONA	1324t	70	16k	554P	47C	12T	BAS	Troon, GB	GB
10	ISLE OF ARRAN	*3296t	84	15k	800P	76C	10T	BA	Port Glasgow, GB	GB
11	ISLE OF CUMBRAE	201t	77	8.5k	160P	15C	–	BA	Troon, GB	GB
12	ISLE OF MULL	*4719t	88	15k	1000P	80C	10T	BA	Port Glasgow, GB	GB
13	JUNO	854t	74	14k	674P	36C	–	AS	Port Glasgow, GB	GB
14	JUPITER	849t	74	14k	658P	36C	–	AS	Port Glasgow, GB	GB
15	LOCH BUIE	*295T	92	8k	250P	10C	–	BA	St Monans, GB	GB
16	LOCH DUNVEGAN	*550t	91	–	250P	36C	–	BA	Port Glasgow, GB	GB
17	LOCH FYNE	*550t	91	–	250P	36C	–	BA	Port Glasgow, GB	GB
18	LOCH LINNHE	*206t	86	8k	203P	12C	–	BA	Hessle, GB	GB
19	LOCH RANZA	*206t	87	8k	203P	12C	–	BA	Hessle, GB	GB
20	LOCH RIDDON	*206t	86	8k	203P	12C	–	BA	Hessle, GB	GB
21	LOCH STRIVEN	*206t	86	8k	203P	12C	–	BA	Hessle, GB	GB
22	LOCH TARBERT	*211t	92	8k	150P	18C	–	BA	St Monans, GB	GB
23p	LOCHMOR	189t	79	10k	130P	0C	–	-	Troon, GB	GB
24	LORD OF THE ISLES	*3504t	89	16k	506P	60C	12L	BAS	Port Glasgow, GB	GB
25	MORVERN	64t	73	8k	142P	4C	–	B	Port Glasgow, GB	GB
26	PIONEER	1071t	74	15k	356P	30C	–	AS	Leith, GB	GB
27	RAASAY	69t	76	8k	164P	6C	–	B	Port Glasgow, GB	GB
28	RHUM	69t	73	8k	164P	6C	–	B	Port Glasgow, GB	GB
29	SATURN	851t	78	14k	694P	36C	–	AS	Troon, GB	GB
30	SUILVEN	1908t	74	15.5k	408P	85C	14L	BA	Moss, NO	GB

BRUERNISH Built for *Caledonian MacBrayne*. Until 1980 she served on a variety of routes. In 1980 she inaugurated RO/RO working between Tayinloan and the island of Gigha and served this route until June 1992 when she was replaced by the LOCH RANZA and become a relief vessel. In summer 1994 she is due to operate as secondary vessel on the Tobermory (Mull) – Kilchoan service.

CALEDONIAN ISLES Built for *Caledonian MacBrayne* for the Ardrossan – Brodick (Arran) service. Entered service on 25th August 1993.

CANNA Built for *Caledonian MacBrayne*. She was the regular vessel on the Lochaline – Fishnish (Mull) service. In 1986 she was replaced by the ISLE OF CUMBRAE and until 1990 she served in a relief capacity in the north, often assisting the MORVERN on the Iona service. In 1990 she replaced the KILBRANNAN (see the ARAINN MHOR, *Maoin-na -Farraige*) on the Kyles Scalpay (Harris) – Scalpay service.

CLAYMORE Built for *Caledonian MacBrayne*. Until 1989 she was generally used on the Oban – Castlebay/ Lochboisdale service, also serving Coll and Tiree from October until May. In 1989 she was transferred to the Kennacraig – Port Ellen/Port Askaig (Islay) route, replacing the IONA. In summer she also operated a weekly service from Port Askaig (Islay) to Colonsay and Oban. She relieved on the Ardrossan – Brodick service during winter 1990. In autumn 1993 she was replaced by the ISLE OF ARRAN and became a spare vessel. Her duties in summer 1994 include 15 Saturday sailings from Ardrossan to Douglas (Isle of Man), returning on Sundays.

COLL Built for *Caledonian MacBrayne*. For several years she was employed mainly in a relief capacity. In 1986 she took over the summer only Tobermory (Mull) – Kilchoan service from a passenger only vessel; the conveyance of vehicles was not inaugurated until 1991.

EIGG Built for *Caledonian MacBrayne*. Since 1976 she has been employed mostly on the Oban – Lismore service.

HEBRIDEAN ISLES Built for *Caledonian MacBrayne* for the Uig – Tarbert/Lochmaddy service. She entered service in December 1985 and was used initially on the Ullapool – Stornoway and Oban – Craignure/Colonsay services pending installation of link-span facilities at Uig, Tarbert and Lochmaddy. She took up her regular role in May 1986.

IONA Built for *David MacBrayne* to operate the Islay service. However, as plans to built a new pier further down West Loch Tarbert were abandoned, she was not able to operate on this route until the *Western Ferries'* pier in deeper water at Kennacraig was acquired in 1978. She operated on the Gourock – Dunoon service in 1970 and 1971, between Mallaig and Kyle of Lochalsh and Stornoway in 1972 and between Oban and Craignure in 1973. From 1974 until 1978 she operated mainly on the Oban to Castlebay/Lochboisdale service. From 1978 until 1989 she operated mainly on the Islay service. In 1989 she was replaced by the CLAYMORE and then replaced the PIONEER as the summer Mallaig – Armadale vessel. She is a relief vessel during the winter. Full RO/RO working was introduced on the route in 1994 and she will also operate a new twice weekly sailing between Mallaig, Lochboisdale and Castlebay.

ISLE OF ARRAN Built for *Caledonian MacBrayne* for the Ardrossan – Brodick service. She has also operated as substitute for the SUILVEN on the Ullapool – Stornoway service. In 1993 transferred to the Kennacraig – Port Ellen/Port Askaig service, also undertaking the weekly Port Askaig – Colonsay – Oban summer service.

ISLE OF CUMBRAE Built for *Caledonian MacBrayne*. Served on the Largs – Cumbrae Slip (Cumbrae) service until 1986 when she was replaced by the LOCH LINNHE and the LOCH STRIVEN and transferred to the Lochaline – Fishnish (Mull) service. She spends most of the winter as secondary vessel on the Kyle of Lochalsh – Kyleakin service.

ISLE OF MULL Built for *Caledonian MacBrayne* to replace the CALEDONIA (1157t, 1966) on the Oban – Craignure (Mull) service. She also operates the Oban – Colonsay service and is the usual relief vessel on the Ullapool – Stornoway service.

JUNO, JUPITER, SATURN Built for *Caledonian MacBrayne* for the Gourock – Dunoon, Gourock – Kilcreggan and Wemyss Bay – Rothesay services. The JUPITER has been upgraded to Class III standard for the Ardrossan – Brodick service. Before 1986, the JUNO and JUPITER operated mainly on the Gourock – Dunoon and Kilcreggan services and the SATURN on the Wemyss Bay – Rothesay service. Between 1986 and 1993 they rotated on a four weekly basis on the three services. In 1993, the SATURN reverted to operating mainly on the Wemyss Bay – Rothesay service. In 1993 certain sailings from Rothesay were extended through the Kyles of Bute to Tighnabruaich on a cruise basis. In 1994 the four weekly rotation was reintroduced and additional cruises will operate in the summer.

LOCH BUIE Built for *Caledonian MacBrayne* for the Fionnphort (Mull) – Iona service to replace the MORVERN and obviate the need for a relief vessel in the summer. Due to height restrictions, loading arrangements for vehicles taller than private cars are bow only .

LOCH DUNVEGAN, LOCH FYNE Built for *Caledonian MacBrayne* for the Kyle of Lochalsh – Kyleakin service, replacing the KYLEAKIN and the LOCHALSH (see *Cross River Ferries*).

LOCH LINNHE Built for *Caledonian MacBrayne* and used mainly on the Largs – Cumbrae Slip (Cumbrae) service. In winter she has been used on the Lochaline – Fishnish service.

LOCH RANZA Built for *Caledonian MacBrayne* and used mainly on the Claonaig – Lochranza (Arran) service. In 1992 she was replaced by the LOCH TARBERT and transferred to the Tayinloan – Gigha service.

LOCH RIDDON Built for *Caledonian MacBrayne* and used mainly on the Colintraive – Rhubodach (Bute) service.

LOCH STRIVEN Built for *Caledonian MacBrayne* and used mainly on the Largs – Cumbrae Slip (Cumbrae) service.

LOCH TARBERT Built for *Caledonian MacBrayne* for the Claonaig – Lochranza (Arran) service. Serves as a relief vessel in the winter.

LOCHMOR Built for *Caledonian MacBrayne* for the passenger only 'small isles' service from Mallaig to Armadale (Skye), Eigg, Muck, Rum and Canna and Kyle of Lochalsh.

LORD OF THE ISLES Built for *Caledonian MacBrayne* to replace the CLAYMORE on the Oban – Castlebay (Barra) and Lochboisdale (South Uist) services and the COLUMBA (1420t, 1964) on the Oban – Coll and Tiree service.

MORVERN Built for *Caledonian MacBrayne*. After service on a number of routes she was, after 1979, the main vessel on the Fionnphort (Mull) – Iona service. In 1992 replaced by the LOCH BUIE and is now a spare vessel.

PIONEER Built for *Caledonian MacBrayne* to operate on the West Loch Tarbert – Port Ellen service (see the IONA). When the IONA was at last able to operate this service in 1978 (following the move to Kennacraig) the PIONEER was transferred to the Mallaig – Armadale service, operating as a spare vessel in the winter. In 1989 she was replaced at Mallaig by the IONA and became the company's spare vessel, replacing the GLEN SANNOX (1269t, 1957). During summer 1994 she will operate additional services on the Wemyss Bay – Rothesay route and will also operate twice weekly between Rothesay and Brodick (Arran) and a 1 hr 30 mins cruise from Brodick

RAASAY Built for *Caledonian MacBrayne* and has been used primarily on the Sconser (Skye) – Raasay service.

RHUM Built for *Caledonian MacBrayne* and, until 1987, used primarily on the Claonaig – Lochranza (Arran) service. Since that time she has served on various routes. In 1994 expected to inaugurate a new service between Tarbert (Loch Fyne) and Portavadie.

SUILVEN Ordered by *A/S Alpha* of Norway for their service across Oslofjord between Moss and Horten and intended to be named the BASTØ VI. However, during construction the order was cancelled and she was completed and launched as the SUILVEN for *Caledonian MacBrayne*. She operates on the Ullapool – Stornoway (Lewis) service. She is due to be replaced in late summer 1995.

Under Construction

31	NEWBUILDING	*c5000t	95	16.5k	1000P	132C	–	BA	Port Glasgow, GB	GB

NEWBUILDING Being built for *Caledonian MacBrayne* to replace the SUILVEN on the Ullapool – Stornoway service.

CROSS RIVER FERRIES

THE COMPANY *Cross River Ferries Ltd* is an Irish Republic company, jointly owned by *Marine Transport Services Ltd* of Cobh and *Arklow Shipping Ltd* of Arklow, County Wicklow.

MANAGEMENT Operations Manager: Edward Perry.

ADDRESS Atlantic Quay, Cobh, County Cork, Republic of Ireland.

TELEPHONE Administration: +353 (0)21 811223, **Reservations:** Not applicable, **Fax:** +353 (0)21 812645.

ROUTE OPERATED Carrigaloe (near Cobh, on Great Island) – Glenbrook (Co Cork) (4 mins; *(1,2)*; frequent service (one or two vessels used according to demand).

VESSELS

1	CARRIGALOE	225t	70	8k	200P	27C	–	BA	Newport (Gwent), GB	IR
2	GLENBROOK	225t	71	8k	200P	27C	–	BA	Newport (Gwent), GB	IR

CARRIGALOE, GLENBROOK Built as the KYLEAKIN and the LOCHALSH for *David MacBrayne Ltd* (later *Caledonian MacBrayne*) for the Kyle of Lochalsh – Kyleakin service. In 1991 replaced by the LOCH DUNVEGAN and the LOCH FYNE and sold to *Marine Transport Services Ltd* who renamed them the CARRIGALOE and the GLENBROOK respectively. They entered service in March 1993.

DOE (NORTHERN IRELAND)

THE COMPANY *DOE (Department of the Environment) (Northern Ireland)* is a UK Department of State.

MANAGEMENT Ferry Manager: H Stephenson.

ADDRESS Strangford Ferries, STRANGFORD, Co Down BT30 7NE.

TELEPHONE Administration: +44 (0)396 881637 **Reservations:** Not applicable. **Fax:** +44 (0)396 881249.

ROUTE OPERATED Strangford – Portaferry (County Down) (10 mins; *(1,2)*; half hourly).

VESSELS

1	PORTAFERRY FERRY	151t	62	9k	200P	22C	–	BA	Pembroke, GB	GB
2	STRANGFORD FERRY	186t	69	10k	263P	22C	–	BA	Cork, IR	GB

PORTAFERRY FERRY Built as the CLEDDAU KING for *Pembrokeshire County Council* (from 1974 *Dyfed County Council*) for their service between Hobbs Point (Pembroke Dock) and Neyland. Following the opening of a new bridge, the service ceased and in 1976 she was sold to *DOE Northern Ireland* and renamed the PORTA FERRY. In 1990 she was renamed the PORTAFERRY FERRY.

STRANGFORD FERRY Built for *Down County Council.* Subsequently transferred to *DOE Northern Ireland.*

GLENELG – KYLERHEA FERRY

THE COMPANY *The Glenelg – Kylerhea Ferry* is privately operated.

MANAGEMENT Ferry Master: R MacLeod.

ADDRESS Corriehallie, Inverinate, KYLE IV40 8HD.

TELEPHONE Administration: +44 (0)59 981 302, **Reservations:** +44 (0)59 981 302, **Fax:** +44 (0)59 981 302.

ROUTE OPERATED Glenelg – Kylerhea (Skye) (summer only) (10 mins; *(1)*; frequent service).

VESSEL

GLENACHULISH	44t	69	9k	12P	6C	–	BSt	Troon, GB	GB

GLENACHULISH Built for the *Ballachulish Ferry Company* for the service between North Ballachulish and South Ballachulish, across the mouth of Loch Leven. In 1975 the ferry was replaced by a bridge and she was sold to *Highland Regional Council* and used on a relief basis on the North Kessock – South Kessock and Kylesku – Kylestrome routes. In 1984 she was sold to the operator of the Glenelg – Kylerhea service. She is the last turntable ferry in operation.

HIGHLAND REGIONAL COUNCIL

THE COMPANY *Highland Regional Council* is a British local government authority.

MANAGEMENT Ferry Manager: J McAulane.

ADDRESS Ferry Cottage, Ardgour, Fort William.

TELEPHONE Administration: +44 (0)85 55 243, **Reservations:** Not applicable. **Fax:** +44 (0)85 55 243.

ROUTE OPERATED Corran – Ardgour (5 mins; *(1 or 2)*; half hourly).

VESSELS

1	MAID OF GLENCOUL	166t	75	8k	116P	16C	–	BA	Ardrossan, GB	GB
2	ROSEHAUGH	150t	67	8.5k	150P	18C	–	BA	Berwick on Tweed, GB/GB

MAID OF GLENCOUL Built for *Highland Regional Council* for the service between Kylesku and Kylestrome. In 1984 the ferry service was replaced by a bridge and she was transferred to the Corran – Ardgour service.

ROSEHAUGH Built for *Ross and Cromarty County Council* for the service between South Kessock and North Kessock (across the Beauly Firth, north of Inverness). In 1975, ownership was transferred to *Highland Regional Council.* In 1982 a bridge was opened and she was transferred to the Corran – Ardgour route. Following the arrival of the MAID OF GLENCOUL in 1984 she has been the reserve vessel.

ISLES OF SCILLY STEAMSHIP COMPANY

THE COMPANY *The Isles of Scilly Steamship Company* is a British private sector company.

MANAGEMENT Managing Director: K N Christopher, **Marketing Manger:** R Johns.

ADDRESS *Scilly:* PO Box 10, HUgh Town, St Mary's, Isles of Scilly TR21 0LJ, *Penzance:* Steamship House, Quay Street, PENZANCE, Cornwall, TR18 4BD.

TELEPHONE Administration & Reservations: *Scilly:* +44 (0)720 22357, *Penzance:* +44 (0)736 64290, **Fax:** *Scilly:* +44 (0)720 22192, *Penzance:* +44 (0)736 51223.

ROUTE OPERATED Penzance – St Mary's (Isles of Scilly) (2 hrs 40 mins; *(1,3)*; 1 per day). Also inter-island services *(2)*.

VESSELS

1	GRY MARITHA	*550t	81	10.5k	12P	5C	1L	C	Kolvereid, NO	GB
2	LYONESSE LADY	*50t	91	9k	12P	1C	0L	A	Fort William, GB	GB
3p	SCILLONIAN III	1256t	77	15.5k	600P	–	-	C	Appledore, GB	GB

GRY MARITHA Built for *Gjofor* of Norway. In design she is a coaster rather than a ferry. In 1990 sold to *The Isles of Scilly Steamship Company.* She operates a freight and passenger service all year (conveying all residents' cars and other vehicles to and from the islands – tourist cars are not conveyed). During the winter she provides the only passenger service to the islands, the SCILLONIAN III being laid up.

Carrigaloe (Miles Cowsill)

Newbuilding (Red Funnel)

LYONESSE LADY Built for *The Isles of Scilly Steamship Company* for inter-island ferry work.

SCILLONIAN III Built for *The Isles of Scilly Steamship Company*. Probably the last 'conventional' passenger/cargo ferry to be built for UK routes. Operates from Easter to late autumn and is laid up in the winter.

MAOIN-NA-FARRAIGE

THE COMPANY *Maoin-Na-Farraige* (literally 'sea treasure' or 'sea wealth') is the trading name for the ferry operations of Udaras na Gaeltacht (The Gaeltacht Authority), a semi-state body responsible for tourism and development in the Irish speaking areas of The Irish Republic.

MANAGEMENT **Managing Director:** Cornelius Bonner.

ADDRESS Bridge House, Leabgarrow, ARRANMORE, County Donegal, Republic of Ireland.

TELEPHONE **Administration & Reservations:** +353 (0)75 21532, **Fax:** + 353 (0)75 21750

ROUTE OPERATED Burtonpoint (County Donegal) – Leabgarrow (Arranmore Island) (20 mins; *(1)*; up to 8 per day).

VESSEL

1	ÁRAINN MHOR	64t	72	8k	50P	4C	–	B	Port Glasgow, GB	GB

ÁRAINN MHOR Built as the KILBRANNAN for *Caledonian MacBrayne*. Used on a variety of routes until 1977, she was then transferred to the Scalpay (Harris) – Kyles Scalpay service. In 1990 she was replaced by the CANNA and, in turn, replaced the CANNA in her reserve/relief role. In 1992 sold to *Maoin-na-Farraige* and renamed the ÁRAINN MHOR.

ORKNEY ISLANDS SHIPPING COMPANY

THE COMPANY *Orkney Islands Shipping Company* is a British company, owned by The Orkney Islands Council.

MANAGEMENT **Operations Director:** R C Sclater, **Ferry Services Manager:** A Learmouth.

ADDRESS 4 Ayres Road, KIRKWALL, Orkney KW15 1QX.

TELEPHONE **Administration:** +44 (0)856 872044, **Reservations:** +44 (0)856 872044, **Fax:** +44 (0)856 872921, **Telex:** 75475.

ROUTES OPERATED Kirkwall (Mainland) to Eday, (1 hr, 15 mins) Westray (1 hr 25 mins), Sanday (1 hr 25 mins), Stronsay (1 hr 35 mins), Westray (1 hr 25 mins), North Ronaldsay (2 hr 30 mins) ('North Isles service')(timings are direct from Kirkwall – sailings via other islands take longer; *(1,2,7)*; daily except Papa Westray which is twice weekly and North Ronaldsay which is weekly), Kirkwall to Shapinsay (25 mins; *(6)*; 6 daily), Houton (Mainland) to Lyness (Hoy) (35 mins *(4)*; 5 daily), Flotta (35 mins *(4)*; 4 daily) and Graemsay (25 mins *(4)*; weekly)('South Isles service') (timings are direct from Houton – sailings via other islands take longer), Tingwall (Mainland) to Rousay (20 mins; *(3)*; 6 daily), Egilsay (30 mins; *(3)*; 5 daily) and Wyre (20 mins; *(3)*; 5 daily) (timings are direct from Tingwall – sailings via other islands take longer).

VESSELS

1	EARL SIGURD	*771t	90	12k	145P	26C	–	BA	Bromborough, GB	GB
2	EARL THORFINN	*771t	90	12k	145P	26C	–	BA	Bromborough, GB	GB
3	EYNHALLOW	*79t	87	9.5k	95P	8C	–	BA	Bristol, GB	GB
4	HOY HEAD	–	94	–	125P	18C	–	BA	Bideford, GB	GB
5	HOY HEAD II	147t	73	9.5k	93P	10C	–	BA	Tórshavn, FA	GB
6	SHAPINSAY	*199t	89	9.5k	91P	12C	–	BA	Hull, GB	GB
7	THORSVOE	*400t	91	10.5k	96P	16C	–	BA	Campbletown, GB	GB
8	VARAGEN	*950t	89	12k	150P	40C	5L	BA	Selby, GB	GB

EARL SIGURD, EARL THORFINN Built for *OISC* to inaugurate RO/RO working on the 'North Isles' service (see above).

EYNHALLOW Built for *OISC* to inaugurate RO/RO services from Tingwall (Mainland) to Rousay, Egilsay and Wyre. In 1991 she was lengthened by 5 metres, to increase car capacity.

HOY HEAD Built for *OISC* to replace the THORSVOE on the 'South Isles' service (see above).

HOY HEAD II Built for *Shetland Islands Council* as the GEIRA and used on their Yell/Unst/Fetlar services until replaced in 1985. In 1986 she was purchased by *OISC* and replaced the LYRAWA BAY (102t, 1970) on the 'South Isles' service (see above). In 1987 she was renamed the HOY HEAD. In 1991 she was replaced by the THORSVOE and became a spare vessel and for sale. On delivery of new HOY HEAD in 1994, renamed HOY HEAD II.

SHAPINSAY Built for *OISC* for the service from Kirkwall (Mainland) to Shapinsay.

THORSVOE Built for *OISC* for the 'South Isles' service (see above). In 1994 replaced by new HOY HEAD and became the main reserve vessel for the fleet.

VARAGEN Built for *Orkney Ferries*, a private company established to start a new route between Gills Bay (Caithness, Scotland) and Burwick (South Ronaldsay, Orkney). However, due to problems with the terminals it was not possible to establish regular services. In 1991, the company was taken over by *OISC* and the VARAGEN became part of their fleet, sharing 'North Isles' services with the EARL SIGURD and the EARL THORFINN and replacing the freight vessel ISLANDER (494t, 1969).

Services are also operated by the GOLDEN MARIANA (33t, 1973), a small passenger vessel.

P&O SCOTTISH FERRIES

THE COMPANY *P&O Scottish Ferries* is British private sector company, part of the *P&O Group*. The name was changed from *P&O Ferries* to *P&O Scottish Ferries* in 1989.

MANAGEMENT Managing Director: T.Cairns, **Marketing Manager:** Stuart Colegate.

ADDRESS PO Box 5, Jamieson's Quay, ABERDEEN AB9 8DL.

TELEPHONE Administration: +44 (0)224589111 Reservations: +44 (0)224 572615, Fax: +44 (0)224 574411. Telex: 73344.

ROUTES OPERATED Scrabster – Stromness (Orkney) (1 hr 45 mins; *(2)*; up to 3 per day)), Aberdeen – Lerwick (Shetland) (14 hrs; *(1)*; up to 6 per week), Aberdeen – Stromness (8 hrs (day), 14 hrs (night)) – Lerwick (8 hrs; *(3)*; 1 per week), Lerwick – Bergen (Norway) (11 hrs; *(3)*;1 per week).

VESSELS

1	ST CLAIR	5700t	71	20k	600P	350C	26L	BA2	Bremerhaven, GE	GB
2	ST OLA	2967t	71	17k	500P	180C	14L	BA	Papenburg, GE	GB
3	ST SUNNIVA	4211t	71	19k	407P	220C	20L	BA	Helsingør, DK	GB

ST CLAIR Built as the TRAVEMÜNDE for *Gedser-Travemünde Ruten* for their service between Gedser (Denmark) and Travemünde (Germany). In 1981 she was sold to *Prekookeanska Plovidba* of Yugoslavia, renamed the NJEGOS and used on their services between Yugoslavia, Greece and Italy. In 1984 chartered to *Sally Line* for use on their Ramsgate- Dunkerque service. In 1985 she was taken on a two year charter by *Brittany Ferries*, renamed the TREGASTEL and moved to the Plymouth – Roscoff service. In 1987 she was purchased and re-registered in France. In 1989 she was replaced by the QUIBERON and transferred to *Truckline Ferries* for their Poole – Cherbourg service. In 1991 she was sold to *P&O Scottish Ferries* and chartered back until winter 1991/2 when she was delivered. Following a major refit she was renamed the ST CLAIR and in March 1992 introduced onto the Aberdeen – Lerwick service, replacing the previous ST CLAIR (4468t, 1965). In addition to operating between Aberdeen and Lerwick, in 1993 she inaugurated a weekly Lerwick – Bergen (Norway) service.

ST OLA Built as the SVEA SCARLETT for *Stockholms Rederi AB Svea* of Sweden and used on the *SL (Skandinavisk Linjetrafik)* service between København (Tuborg Havn) and Landskrona (Sweden). In 1980 she was sold to *Scandinavian Ferry Lines* of Sweden and *Dampskibsselskabet Øresund A/S* of Denmark (jointly owned). Initially she continued to serve Landskrona but later that year the Swedish terminal became Malmö. In 1981 she operated on the Helsingborg – Helsingør service for a short while, after which she was withdrawn and laid up. In 1982 she was sold to *Eckerö Line* of Finland, renamed the ECKERÖ and used on services between Grisslehamn (Sweden) and Eckerö (Åland Islands). In 1991 she was sold to *P&O Scottish Ferries* and renamed

St. Clair (Lawrence MacDuff)

the ST OLA. In March 1992 she replaced the previous ST OLA (1345t, 1974) on the Scrabster – Stromness service.

ST SUNNIVA Built as the DJURSLAND for *Jydsk Faergefart* of Denmark for their service between Grenå (Jutland) and Hundested (Sealand). In 1974 she was replaced by a larger vessel called DJURSLAND II (4371t, 1974) and switched to the company's other route, between Juelsminde (Jutland) and Kalundborg (Sealand), being renamed the LASSE II. In 1979 she was sold to *P&O Ferries*, renamed the N F PANTHER ('N F' standing for '*Normandy Ferries*') and became the third vessel on the Dover – Boulogne service. Sold to *European Ferries* in 1985 and in summer 1986 replaced (with sister vessel NF TIGER (4045t, 1972)) by the FREE ENTERPRISE IV (5049t, 1969) and FREE ENTERPRISE V (5044t, 1970). In 1987 sold to *P&O Ferries*, renamed the ST SUNNIVA, converted to an overnight ferry and introduced onto the Aberdeen – Lerwick service, supplementing ST CLAIR and also providing a weekly Aberdeen – Stromness – Lerwick – and return service.

PASSAGE EAST FERRY

THE COMPANY *Passage East Ferry Company Ltd* is an Irish Republic private sector company.

MANAGEMENT Managing Director: Mr B Donnelly.

ADDRESS 18 Parnell St, Waterford, Republic of Ireland.

TELEPHONE Administration: +353 (0)51 74203. Reservations: Not applicable.

ROUTE OPERATED Passage East (County Waterford) – Ballyhack (County Wexford) (10 mins; *(1)*; frequent service).

VESSEL

F.B.D. DUNBRODY	139t	60	8k	120P	18C	–	BA	Hamburg, GE	IR

F.B.D. DUNBRODY Built as the BERNE-FARGE for the service between Berne and Farge, across the River Weser in Germany. Subsequently she was sold to *Elbe Clearing* of Germany, renamed the ELBE CLEARING 12 and used as a floating platform for construction works in the Elbe. In 1979 she was sold to *Passage East Ferry Company* and renamed the F.B.D. DUNBRODY. Passenger capacity is 70 in the winter.

RED FUNNEL FERRIES

THE COMPANY *Red Funnel Ferries* is the trading name of the *Southampton Isle of Wight and South of England Royal Mail Steam Packet Public Limited Company*, a British private sector company. The company was acquired by *Associated British Ports* (owners of Southampton Docks) in 1989.

MANAGEMENT Managing Director: A M Whyte, Marketing Director: Ms O H Glass.

ADDRESS 12 Bugle Street, SOUTHAMPTON SO9 4LJ.

TELEPHONE Administration: +44 (0)703 333042, Reservations: +44 (0)703 330333, Fax: +44 (0)703 639438.

ROUTE OPERATED Southampton – East Cowes (1 hr; *(1,2,3,4)*; hourly).

VESSELS

1	COWES CASTLE	912t	65	12k	866P	65C	16L	BA	Southampton, GB	GB
2	NETLEY CASTLE	1184t	74	12k	786P	85C	16L	BA	Wallsend, GB	GB
3	NORRIS CASTLE	922t	68	12k	866P	65C	16L	BA	Southampton, GB	GB
4	RED FALCON	*3000t	94	13k	900P	140C	14L	BA	Port Glasgow, GB	GB

COWES CASTLE, NORRIS CASTLE Built for *Red Funnel*. Lengthened and converted from bow loading to through deck loading during winter 1975/6. Passenger capacity quoted above is for the summer. In the winter it is reduced to 599 for the COWES CASTLE and 628 for the NORRIS CASTLE. Due to be withdrawn in 1994.

NETLEY CASTLE Built for *Red Funnel*. Although largely built at Wallsend, she was completed at Southampton as her original builders went bankrupt. Passenger capacity quoted above is for the summer. In the winter it is reduced to 715.

RED FALCON Built for *Red Funnel Ferries* to replace the COWES CASTLE.

Under construction

NEWBUILDING	*3000t	95	13k	900P	140C	14L	BA	Port Glasgow, GB	GB

NEWBUILDING Being built for *Red Funnel Ferries* to replace the NORRIS CASTLE.

Red Funnel Ferries also operate two 67 passenger hydrofoils named the SHEARWATER 5 (62t, 1980) and the SHEARWATER 6 (62t, 1982) and two 130 passenger catamarans named the RED JET 1 (168t, 1991) and the RED JET 2 (168t, 1991). They operate between Southampton and West Cowes; journey time is 20 minutes.

SHANNON FERRY LTD

THE COMPANY *Shannon Ferry Ltd* is an Irish Republic private company owned by six families on both sides of the Shannon Estuary.

MANAGEMENT Manager: Michael F O'Sullivan.

ADDRESS Killimer, County Clare, Republic of Ireland.

TELEPHONE Administration: +353 (0)65 53124. **Reservations:** Not applicable.

ROUTE OPERATED Killimer (County Clare) – Tarbert (County Kerry) (20 mins; *(1,2)*; hourly (generally only one vessel used)).

VESSELS

1	SHANNON HEATHER	300t	68	9k	250P	30C	–	BA	Dartmouth, GB	IR
2	SHANNON WILLOW	360t	78	10k	300P	44C	–	BA	Bowling, GB	IR

SHANNON HEATHER, SHANNON WILLOW Built for *Shannon Ferry*.

Hendra (Ferry Publications Library)

SHETLAND ISLANDS COUNCIL

THE COMPANY *Shetland Islands Council* is a British Local Government authority.

MANAGEMENT Director of Marine Operations: Capt G H Sutherland, FNI MRIN.

ADDRESS Port Administration Building, Sella Ness, MOSSBANK, Shetland ZE2 9QR.

TELEPHONE Administration: +44 (0)806 242551, **Reservations:** +44 (0)95 782 268. **Fax:** +44 (0)806 242237. **Telex:** 75142 Sulvoe G.

ROUTES OPERATED Toft (Mainland) – Ulsta (Yell) (20 mins; *(1,5)*; up to 26 per day), Gutcher (Yell) – Belmont (Unst) (10 mins; *(3)*; 30 per day), Gutcher (Yell) – Oddsta (Fetlar) (25 mins; *(4)*; 6 per day), Lerwick (Mainland) – Bressay (5 mins; *(11)*; 19 per day), Laxo (Mainland) – Symbister (Whalsay) (30 mins; *(8,9)*; 17 per day), Lerwick (Mainland) – Out Skerries (3 hrs; *(2)*; 2 per week), Vidlin (Mainland) – Out Skerries (1 hrs 30 mins; *(2)*; 7 per week), Grutness (Mainland) – Fair Isle (3 hrs; *(6)*; 2 per week), West Burrafirth (Mainland) – Papa Stour (40 mins; *(10)*; 7 per week), West Burrafirth (Mainland) – Foula (3 hrs; *(13)*; 2 per week).

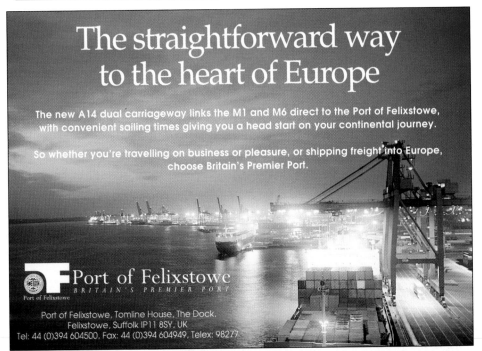
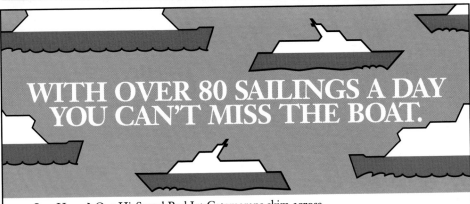

VESSELS

1	BIGGA	*274t	91	11k	96P	21C	4L	BA	St Monans, GB	GB
2	FILLA	*130t	83	9k	12P	6C	1T	A	Flekkefjord, NO	GB
3	FIVLA	*230t	85	11k	95P	15C	4L	BA	Troon, GB	GB
4	FYLGA	147t	75	8.5k	93P	10C	2L	BA	Tórshavn, FA	GB
5	GEIRA	*226t	88	10.8k	95P	15C	4L	BA	Hessle, GB	GB
6	GOOD SHEPHERD IV	*76t	86	10k	12P	1C	0L	C	St Monans, GB	GB
7	GRIMA	147t	74	8.5k	93P	10C	2L	BA	Bideford, GB	GB
8	HENDRA	225t	82	11k	100P	18C	4L	BA	Bromborough, GB	GB
9	KJELLA	158t	57	10.5k	63P	12C	2L	BA	Harstad, NO	GB
10	KOADA	35t	69	8k	12P	1C	0L	C	Bideford, GB	GB
11	LEIRNA	*420t	93	10k	100P	20C	4L	BA	Greenock, GB	GB
12	THORA	147t	75	8.5k	93P	10C	2L	BA	Tórshavn, FA	GB

BIGGA Built for *Shetland Islands Council* and used on the Toft (Mainland) – Ulsta (Yell) service.

FILLA Built for *Shetland Islands Council*. Used on the Lerwick (Mainland) – Out Skerries and Vidlin (Mainland) – Out Skerries services. At other times she operates freight services around the Shetland Archipelago. She resembles a miniature oil rig supply vessel.

FIVLA Built for *Shetland Islands Council*. Used on the Gutcher (Yell) – Belmont (Unst) service.

FYLGA Built for *Shetland Islands Council*. Now used on the Gutcher (Yell) – Oddsta (Fetlar) service.

GEIRA Built for *Shetland Islands Council*. Now used on the Toft (Mainland) – Ulsta (Yell) service.

GOOD SHEPHERD IV Built for *Shetland Islands Council*. Used on the service between Grutness (Mainland) and Fair Isle. Vehicles conveyed by special arrangement and generally consist of agricultural vehicles for the islanders.

GRIMA Built for *Shetland Islands Council*. Used on the Lerwick (Mainland) – Maryfield (Bressay) service until 1992 when she was replaced by the LEIRNA and became a spare vessel.

HENDRA Built for *Shetland Islands Council*. Used on the Laxo (Mainland) – Symbister (Whalsay) service.

KJELLA Built for *A/S Torghatten Trafikkselskap* of Norway for Norwegian fjord services. In 1980 purchased by *Shetland Islands Council*. She operates on the Laxo (Mainland) – Symbister (Whalsay) service.

KOADA Built as an inshore trawler and bought by the shareholders on Fair Isle to operate to Shetland and named the GOOD SHEPHERD III. In 1986 the service was taken over by *Shetland Islands Council* and she was replaced by GOOD SHEPHERD IV. She was however acquired by the Council and renamed the KOADA. She now operates between West Burrafirth (Mainland) and Papa Stour and Foula. Car carrying capacity used occasionally. When the new Foula vessel is delivered in May 1994 she will serve Papa Stour only.

LEIRNA Built for *Shetland Islands Council* for the Lerwick – Maryfield (Bressay) service. She is of similar design to *Caledonian MacBrayne's* LOCH DUNVEGAN and LOCH FYNE.

THORA Built for *Shetland Islands Council*. Now a spare vessel. Sister vessel to the FYLGA and the GRIMA,

UNDER CONSTRUCTION

13	NEWBUILDING	–	94	–	12P	1C	–	C	Southampton, GB	GB

NEWBUILDING Under construction for the FOULA service. She will be based on the island and, when not in use, hoisted out of the water by a Watercraft Schat PHA Davit. She is not a car ferry but can convey 9 tons of cargo and will therefore be able to carry a vehicle for use on the island.

SEABOARD MARINE (NIGG)

THE COMPANY *Seaboard Marine (Nigg)* is a British private company.

MANAGEMENT **Managing Director:** Andrew Thoms, **Marketing Manager:** Robert McCrae.

ADDRESS Cliff House, Cadboll, TAIN, Ross-shire.

TELEPHONE **Administration:** +44 (0)86 287 254, **Reservations:** +44 (0)86 285 324, **Fax:** +44 (0)86 287 231.

ROUTE OPERATED Cromarty – Nigg (Ross-shire) (10 mins; *(1)*; half hourly).

VESSEL

CROMARTY ROSE	28t	87	8k	50P	2C	–	B	Ardrossan, GB	GB

CROMARTY ROSE Built for *Seaboard Marine (Nigg)*.

STRATHCLYDE REGIONAL COUNCIL

THE COMPANY *Strathclyde Regional Council* is a British local government authority.

MANAGEMENT **Area Engineer:** James C Tolmie.

ADDRESS Strathclyde Roads, North Argyll, Kilbowie House, Gallanach Road, OBAN PA34 4PF.

TELEPHONE **Administration:** +44 (0)631 62125 **Reservations:** +44 (0)631 62125, **Fax:** +44 (0)631 66728.

ROUTE OPERATED Seil – Luing (5 mins; *(1)*; frequent service).

VESSEL

BELNAHUA	35t	72	8k	40P	5C	1L	BA	Campbeltown, GB	GB

BELNAHUA Built for *Argyll County Council* for the Seil – Luing service. In 1975, following local government reorganisation, transferred to *Strathclyde Regional Council*.

WESTERN FERRIES (ARGYLL)

THE COMPANY *Western Ferries (Argyll)* is a British private sector company, a subsidiary of Harrisons (Clyde) Ltd.

MANAGEMENT Managing Director: A Wilson.

ADDRESS 16 Woodside Crescent, GLASGOW G3 7UT.

TELEPHONE Administration: +44 (0)41-332 9766. **Reservations:** Not applicable. **Fax:** +44 (0)41-332 0267, **Telex:** 77203.

ROUTE OPERATED Port Askaig (Islay) – Feolin (Jura) (5 mins; *(1)*; approx hourly).

VESSEL

1	SOUND OF GIGHA	65t	66	7.5k	28P	8C	–	BA	Bideford, GB	GB

SOUND OF GIGHA Built as the ISLE OF GIGHA for *Eilean Sea Service*. She was built as small 'landing-craft' type vessel, conveying lorries around the west coast of Scotland. In 1969, purchased by *Western Ferries*, converted to a car and passenger vessel, renamed the SOUND OF GIGHA and put onto the Port Askaig (Islay) – Feolin (Jura) service.

St Cecilia (Miles Cowsill)

Sound of Seil (John Hendy)

WESTERN FERRIES (CLYDE)

THE COMPANY

Western Ferries (Clyde) is a British private sector company. The company broke away from *Western Ferries (Argyll)* following a management 'buy out' in 1985.

MANAGEMENT Managing Director: Alan Bradley,

ADDRESS Hunter's Quay, DUNOON PA23 8HY.

TELEPHONE Administration: +44 (0)369 4452, **Reservations:** Not applicable, **Fax:** +44 (0)369 6020, **Telex:** +44 (0)41-332 0267.

ROUTE OPERATED McInroy's Point, Gourock – Hunter's Quay, Dunoon (20 mins; *(1,2,3,4)*; half hourly).

VESSELS

1	SOUND OF SCARBA	175t	60	7k	200P	22C	–	BA	Åmål, SW	GB
2	SOUND OF SEIL	363t	59	10.5k	620P	26C	–	BA	Troon, GB	GB
3	SOUND OF SHUNA	244t	62	7k	200P	25C	–	BA	Åmål, SW	GB
4	SOUND OF SLEAT	466t	61	10k	296P	30C	–	BAS	Hardinxveld, NL	GB

SOUND OF SCARBA Built as the ÖLANDSSUND III for *Rederi AB Ölandssund* of Sweden for service between Revsudden on the mainland and Stora Rör on the island of Öland. Following the opening of a new bridge near Kalmar, about 4 miles to the South, the ferry service ceased. In 1973 she was sold to *Western Ferries*, renamed the SOUND OF SCARBA and joined the SOUND OF SHUNA their Gourock – Dunoon service. Now relief vessel and also used on contract work in the Clyde estuary.

SOUND OF SEIL Built as the FRESHWATER for *British Railways* for their Lymington – Yarmouth (Isle of Wight) service. In 1983 sold to Lebanese interests for an undisclosed purpose but remained laid up at Portsmouth until 1985 when she was sold to *Western Ferries*. In 1986 she was renamed the SOUND OF SEIL and introduced on the Gourock – Dunoon service.

SOUND OF SHUNA Built as the ÖLANDSSUND IV for *Rederi AB Ölandssund* of Sweden (see the SOUND OF SCARBA above). In 1973 she was sold to *Western Ferries*, renamed the SOUND OF SHUNA and, with the SOUND OF SCARBA, inaugurated the Gourock – Dunoon service.

SOUND OF SLEAT Built as the DE HOORN for the service between Maassluis and Rozenburg, across the 'Nieuwe Waterweg' (New Waterway) in The Netherlands. In 1988 she was purchased by *Western Ferries (Clyde)*, renamed the SOUND OF SLEAT and introduced onto the Gourock – Dunoon service.

WESTERN ISLES ISLANDS COUNCIL

THE COMPANY *Western Isles Islands Council* is a British municipal authority.

ADDRESS Council Offices, Sandwick Road, STORNOWAY, Isle of Lewis PA87 2BW.

TELEPHONE Administration: +44 (0)851 703773, Extn 490. Reservations: *Berneray Ferry:* +44 (0)87 67 230, *Eriskay Ferry:* +44 (0)87 86 261, Fax: +44 (0)851 705349.

ROUTE OPERATED Ludaig (South Uist) – Eriskay (30 mins; *(2)*; 3 per day (minimum)), Newtonferry (North Uist) – Berneray (15 mins; *(1)*; 5 per day (minimum)). Additional services operate during the summer.

VESSELS

| 1 | EILEAN BHEARNARAIGH | 67t | 83 | 7k | 35P | 4C | 1T | BA | Glasgow, GB | GB |
| 2 | EILEAN NA H-OIGE | 69t | 80 | 7k | 35P | 4C | 1T | BA | Stornoway, GB | GB |

EILEAN BHEARNARAIGH Built for *Western Isles Islands Council* for their Newtonferry (North Uist) – Berneray service.

EILEAN NA H-OIGE Built for *Western Isles Islands Council* for their Ludaig (South Uist) – Eriskay service.

WIGHTLINK

THE COMPANY *Wightlink* is a British private sector company, part of the *Sea Containers* group. The routes and vessels were previously part of *Sealink* but were excluded from the purchase of most of the *Sealink* operations by *Stena Line AB* in 1990.

MANAGEMENT Managing Director: Mel Williams, Marketing Manager: R I Stewart.

ADDRESS PO Box 59, PORTSMOUTH PO1 2XB.

TELEPHONE Administration: +44 (0)705 812011, Reservations: +44 (0)705 827744, Fax: +44 (0)705 855257, Telex: 86440 WIGHTLG.

ROUTES OPERATED Lymington – Yarmouth (Isle of Wight) (30 mins; *(1,2,3)*; half hourly), Portsmouth – Fishbourne (Isle of Wight) (35 mins; *(4,5,6)*; half hourly/hourly).

VESSELS

1	CAEDMON	761t	73	9.5k	756P	58C	6L	BA	Dundee, GB	GB
2	CENRED	761t	73	9.5k	756P	58C	6L	BA	Dundee, GB	GB
3	CENWULF	761t	73	9.5k	756P	58C	6L	BA	Dundee, GB	GB
4	ST CATHERINE	*2036t	83	12.5k	1000P	142C	12L	BA	Leith, GB	GB
5	ST CECILIA	*2968t	87	12.5k	1000P	142C	12L	BA	Selby, GB	GB
6	ST FAITH	*2968t	90	12.5k	1000P	142C	12L	BA	Selby, GB	GB
7	ST HELEN	*2983t	83	12.5k	1000P	142C	12L	BA	Leith, GB	GB

ST CATHERINE, ST CECILIA, ST FAITH, ST HELEN Built for the Portsmouth – Fishbourne service. The ST HELEN is currently laid up.

CAEDMON Built for Portsmouth – Fishbourne service. In 1983 transferred to the Lymington – Yarmouth service.

CENRED, CENWULF Built for Lymington – Yarmouth service.

Wightlink also operate two passenger only high speed catamarans – the OUR LADY PATRICIA and the OUR LADY PAMELA – between Portsmouth and Ryde. They are of 312 tons, were built in 1986 in Tasmania, Australia, seat 406 passengers, cruise at 28.5k and are British registered.

WOOLWICH FREE FERRY

THE COMPANY The *Woolwich Free Ferry* is operated by the *London Borough of Greenwich*, a British municipal authority.

MANAGEMENT **Principal Engineer:** J R Parker, **Ferry Manager:** Capt P Deeks.

ADDRESS New Ferry Approach, Woolwich, LONDON SE18 6DX.

TELEPHONE **Administration:** +44 (0)81-854 3488, **Reservations:** Not applicable, **Fax:** +44 (0)81-316 6096.

ROUTE OPERATED Woolwich – North Woolwich (free ferry) (5 mins; *(1,2,3)*; 5 mins (weekdays), 10 mins (weekends)).

VESSELS

1	ERNEST BEVIN	738t	63	–	300P	32C	6L	BA	Dundee, GB,	GB
2	JAMES NEWMAN	738t	63	–	300P	32C	6L	BA	Dundee, GB,	GB
3	JOHN BURNS	738t	63	–	300P	32C	6L	BA	Dundee, GB,	GB

ERNEST BEVIN, JAMES NEWMAN, JOHN BURNS Built for the *London County Council* who operated the service in 1963. In 1965 ownership was transferred to the *Greater London Council*. Following the abolition of the *GLC* in April 1986, ownership was transferred to the *Department of Transport*. The *London Borough of Greenwich* operate the service on their behalf.

SECTION 4 – FREIGHT ONLY FERRIES

BELFAST FREIGHT FERRIES

THE COMPANY *Belfast Freight Ferries* is a British private sector company owned by *Scruttons plc* of London.

MANAGEMENT Operations Director: Trevor Wright. Commercial Director: Alan Peacock.

ADDRESS Victoria Terminal 1, Dargan Road, BELFAST BT3 9LJ.

TELEPHONE Administration: +44 (0)232 770112. Reservations: +44 (0)232 770112. Fax: +44 (0)232 781217.

ROUTE OPERATED Heysham – Belfast; (8 hours; *(1,2,3)*; 3 daily)

VESSELS

1	RIVER LUNE	2826t	83	16k	12P	–	80T	A	Galatz, RO	BA
2	SAGA MOON	*6564t	84	15.5k	12P	–	62T	A	Travemünde, GE	GI
3	SPHEROID	7171t	71	16k	12P	–	52T	A	Sharpsborg, NO	IM

RIVER LUNE Built for chartering as the BALDER VIK and initially used on services between Italy and the Middle East. Subsequently she was employed on a number of charters including *North Sea Ferries* and *Norfolk Line*. In 1986 she was sold to *Navrom* of Romania, renamed the BAZIAS 7 and initially used on their Mediterranean and Black Sea services. In 1987 she was chartered to *Kent Line* for service between Chatham and Zeebrugge. In 1988 she was sold to *Stena AB* of Sweden and chartered for service between Finland and Germany. In 1989 she was briefly renamed the STENA TOPPER before being further renamed the SALAR. During the ensuing years she undertook a number of charters. In 1993 chartered to *Belfast Freight Ferries* and renamed the RIVER LUNE.

SAGA MOON Built as the LIDARTINDUR for *Trader Line* of the Faroe Islands for services between Tórshavn and Denmark. In 1986 chartered to *Belfast Freight Ferries* renamed the SAGA MOON.

SPHEROID Built as the STARMARK for *Avermoi Oy* of Finland. In 1981 sold to *Manta Line* of Greece for Mediterranean and deep sea service and renamed the RORO TRADER. In 1985 she was sold to *Oceanwide Shipping* for charter and renamed the NIEKIRK. In 1986 chartered to *Belfast Freight Ferries* and in 1987 sold to them and renamed the SPHEROID.

COBELFRET RO/RO SERVICES

THE COMPANY *Cobelfret RO/RO Services* is a Belgian private sector company, a subsidiary of *Cobelfret nv* of Antwerp.

MANAGEMENT Managing Director (Belgium): George Bruers, Managing Director (UK): Mike Gray, UK Agents: Ronnie Daelman and Peter Mann (Purfleet Agencies).

Spirit of Boulogne (Miles Cowsill)

Newbuilding - (Commodore)

ADDRESS *(Belgium)* Sneeuwbeslaan 14 B2610, ANTWERP, Belgium, *UK:* Purfleet Thames Terminal Ltd, London Road, PURFLEET, Essex RM16 1RT.

TELEPHONE Administration *Belgium:* +32 (0)3 829 9011, *UK:* +44 (0)708 865522, **Reservations** *UK:* +44 (0)708 891199, **Fax:** *Belgium:* +32 (0)3 237 7646, *UK (Admin):* +44 (0)708 866418, *UK (Reservations):* +44 (0)708 890853, **Telex:** *Belgium:* 32600, *UK (Admin):* 897854, *UK (Reservations):* 911683

ROUTES OPERATED Zeebrugge – Purfleet (8 hrs; 4 per day), Zeebrugge – Immingham (14 hrs; 9 per week). Vessels are switched between routes (and other *Cobelfret* services not serving the UK), so it is not possible so say which vessels serve on which routes at any particular time.

VESSELS

1	BELVAUX	6832t	79	14k	12P	520C	100T	R	Hoboken, BE	LX
2	CYMBELINE	*11886t	92	14.5k	10P	790C	130T	A2	Dalian, CH	PA
3	EGLANTINE	*10030t	89	14.5k	10P	790C	120T	A2	Dalian, CH	PA
4	LOVERVAL	5580t	78	17k	12P	675C	112T	A2	Lödöse, SW	LX
5	NORDBORG	5326t	79	16k	12P	400C	130T	A2	Lödöse, SW	DK
6	SYMPHORINE	*9059t	88	14.5k	10P	790C	130T	A2	Dalian, CH	PA
7	UNDINE	*11854t	91	14.5k	10P	790C	130T	A2	Dalian, CH	PA

BELVAUX Built for *Cobelfret.*

CYMBELINE Built for *Cobelfret.*

EGLANTINE Built by *Cobelfret.*

LOVERVAL Built as the VALLMO for the *Johansson Group* of Sweden and undertook a variety of charters. In 1982 she was sold Cobelfret and renamed the MATINA. In 1984 renamed the LOVERVAL.

NORDBORG Built as the LINNÉ and chartered to *OT Africa Line* for services between Italy and Lybia. In 1985 sold and renamed the BELINDA; she was employed on a variety of charters including *DFDS* and *Stena Line* until 1988 when she was sold to *Dannebrog* of Denmark and renamed the NORDBORG. Chartering continued, including *Kent Line* and *DFDS* again, and in 1993 she was chartered to *Cobelfret.*

SYMPHORINE Built *Cobelfret.*

UNDINE Built for *Cobelfret.*

COMMODORE FERRIES

THE COMPANY *Commodore Ferries Ltd* is a Guernsey private sector company.

MANAGEMENT **Managing Director:** Jeff Vidamour.

ADDRESS Commodore House, Bulwer Avenue, St Sampson's, GUERNSEY, Channel Islands GY2 4JN.

TELEPHONE **Administration:** +44 (0)481 46841 **Reservations:** +44 (0)481 46841. **Fax:** +44 (0)481 49543.

ROUTE OPERATED Portsmouth – Channel Islands (9 hrs; *(1,2,3)*; 3 per day).

VESSELS

1	COMMODORE CLIPPER	2311t	71	17k	12P	–	50T	A	Kristiansand, NO	NO
2	NORMAN COMMODORE	1577t	72	17k	12P	–	45T	BA	Florø, NO	BA
3	PURBECK	*3046t	78	17.5k	58P	–	64T	BA	Le Havre, FR	FR

COMMODORE CLIPPER Built as the JUNO. In 1979 sold to *Finnfranline* of France, renamed the NORMANDIA and chartered to *Finncarriers* for service between Finland and France. In 1982 chartered to *Sucargo* and used on services between France and Algeria and the Middle East. In 1986 sold to *Mikkola* of Finland, renamed the MISIDIA and chartered to *Transfennica* for services between Finland and Northern Europe. In 1990 sold to *Kristiania Ejendom* of Norway and renamed the EURO NOR. In 1991 she was chartered to *Commodore Ferries* and renamed the COMMODORE CLIPPER.

NORMAN COMMODORE Built as the ANU for *Alander Franchtschiff oy* of Finland for the charter market. In 1973 she was chartered to *North Sea Ferries* and renamed the NORCLIFF. She reverted to her original name in 1974. In 1980 she was chartered to *Sealink UK Ltd* and after a short period on the Fishguard – Rosslare service, she was transferred to the Heysham – Belfast freight service where she was renamed LUNE BRIDGE. This service ceased in December of that year and she was then chartered to *B&I Line*, being renamed the LADY CATHERINE, and used on the Dublin – Holyhead service. In 1981 she was chartered to *Lakespan Marine* of Canada for service on the Great Lakes and renamed the LAKESPAN ONTARIO. In 1983 she was chartered to the British *Ministry of Defence* for *Royal Fleet Auxiliary* service to replace the SIR TRISTRAM, which had been lost in the Falklands campaign. She was renamed the SIR LAMORAK. In 1986 she was chartered to *Merchant Ferries*, renamed the MERCHANT TRADER and used on the Heysham – Warrenpoint service. In 1987 chartered to *Mols Line* of Denmark for service between Ebeltoft (Jutland) and Sjaellands Odde (Sealand). She was initially renamed the MOLS TRADER and then the MADS MOLS. In 1989 she was chartered to *Mainland Market Deliveries* of Great Britain to operate a new service between Portsmouth and the Channel Islands and renamed the PRIDE OF PORTSMOUTH. In 1990, *Commodore Ferries*, a long established Channel Islands operator, switched from LO/LO to RO/RO operations and absorbed this operation. In 1991 she was renamed the NORMAN COMMODORE. In late 1993 she suffered a serious fire and was temporarily replaced by the JUNIPER (1575t, 1977 (ex CAP BENAT 1986)).

PURBECK Built for *Truckline Ferries* for their Cherbourg – Poole service. In 1986 she was stretched to increase vehicle capacity by 24%. In 1992 transferred to the Roscoff – Plymouth and Santander – Plymouth services. In 1994 chartered to *British Channel Island Ferries* to operate freight services between Poole and The Channel Islands. In 1994, charter transferred to *Commodore Ferries* following the cessation of *BCIF's* operations.

Under construction

NEWBUILDING	–	95	18.3k	12P	–	95T	A	Vlissingen, NL	BA

NEWBUILDING Under construction for *Commodore Ferries* to replace the NORMAN COMMODORE.

DFDS

THE COMPANY *DFDS* is one of the trading names of the freight division of *DFDS A/S*, a Danish private sector public company. See also *Tor Line* (Swedish services).

MANAGEMENT Managing Director UK: Ebbe Pederson.

ADDRESS Scandinavia House, Parkeston Quay, HARWICH CO12 4QG.

TELEPHONE Administration & Reservations: +44 (0)255 242242, **Fax:** +44 (0)255 244310, **Telex:** 98582.

ROUTES OPERATED Grimsby – Esbjerg (20 hrs; *(1,3)*; 4 per week), North Shields – Esbjerg (24 hrs; *(1,3)*; 2 per week), Immingham – Cuxhaven (22 hrs: *(2,4)* 5 per week) (under the name of *Elbe – Humber RoLine*), Harwich – Esbjerg (20 hrs; *(3)*; 6 per week (including sailings by passenger vessel DANA ANGLIA)).

VESSELS

#	Name	Tonnage	Year	Speed							
1	DANA CIMBRIA	*12189t	86	17.5k	12P	–	150T	A	Frederikshavn, DK	DK
2	DANA CORONA	4301t	72	16k	12P	–	100T	A	Rauma, FI	NO
3	DANA MAXIMA	4928t	78	18k	12P	–	178T	A	Nagasu, JA	DK
4	FICHTELBERG	3973t	75	18.5k	12P	–	94T	A	Kristiansand, NO	GE
5	TOR DANIA	8670t	78	16k	12P	–	94T	AS	Dunkerque, FR	SW

DANA CIMBRIA Launched as the MERCANDIAN EXPRESS II and immediately bareboat chartered to *DFDS* for their North Sea freight services, being renamed the DANA CIMBRIA. Generally used on the Grimsby and North Shields services.

DANA CORONA Built as the ANTARES for *Finska Ångfartygs A/B* of Finland and used on services between Finland and Germany. In 1975 she was renamed the RHEINFELS. In 1977 she was sold to *Nedlloyd* of the Netherlands and renamed the NEDLLOYD ROCKANJE. In the early eighties she was chartered to *Constellation Line* of the USA for services between the USA and Europe. In 1983 she was sold to *Kotka Line* of Finland, renamed the KOTKA LILY and used on their services between Finland, UK and West Africa. In 1985 she was chartered to *Jahre Line* of Norway, renamed the JALINA and operated freight services between Oslo and Kiel. Two years later, she returned to Baltic waters, being chartered to *Finncarriers* and renamed the FINNROVER. In 1988 she was chartered to *Kent Line*, renamed the SEAHORSE and used on their Dartford – Zeebrugge service. In 1991 she was chartered to *DFDS* and in 1992 she was renamed the DANA CORONA. She is used on the service between the Immingham and Cuxhaven (Germany) operated in the name of *Elbe Humber RoLine*.

DANA MAXIMA Built for *DFDS* for their North Sea services. Generally used on the Grimsby and North Shields services.

FICHTELBERG Launched as the TOR CALEDONIA for *Tor Line* of Sweden for North Sea service. In 1978 sold to *DSR Line* of the former DDR and renamed the FICHTELBERG. She was used on services between the DDR and Cuba and also performed a number of charters. In 1991 she was chartered to *Dublin Ferries* for a new Dublin-Liverpool service and in 1992 she was renamed the SPIRIT OF DUBLIN. Later in 1992 the service cased and, after a brief period with her owners, resuming the name FICHTELBERG, she was chartered to *North Sea Ferries* and placed on the Hull – Rotterdam service, being renamed NORCLIFF. In 1993 the charter was ended and she returned to her owners and resumed her name. In 1994 chartered to *DFDS* to provide additional capacity of the Immingham – Cuxhaven service following the ending of *DSR Line's* service between Hull and Hamburg.

European Clearway (FotoFlite)

TOR DANIA Built as the VILLE DE DUNKERQUE for *Société Française de Transports Maritimes* of France. Between 1979 and 1981 she was renamed the FOSS DUNKERQUE. In 1986 she was chartered to *Grimaldi Line* of Italy and renamed the G AND C EXPRESS. In 1988 she was briefly was briefly renamed the RAILO and then she was chartered to *DFDS* where she was renamed the DANIA HAFNIA. The following year she was chartered to *Maersk Line* of Denmark, renamed the MAERSK ESSEX and used on *Kent Line* services between Dartford and Zeebrugge. In 1992 she was chartered to and later purchased by *DFDS* and renamed the TOR DANIA. In 1993 she was renamed the BRIT DANIA but later in the year reverted to her original name. She is generally used on the Harwich – Esbjerg service, working in consort with the passenger ferry DANIA ANGLIA (see *Scandinavian Seaways*).

EIMSKIP

THE COMPANY *Eimskip* is an Icelandic private sector company.

ADDRESS Reykjavik, Iceland.

TELEPHONE Administration: +354 (0)1 697100. Reservations: *Iceland:* +354 (0)1 697100, *UK:* +44 (0)469 571880, Fax: *Iceland:* +354 (0)1 28216, *UK:* +44 (0)469 571318, Telex: *Iceland:* 2022, *UK:* 527179.

ROUTE OPERATED Reykjavik – Immingham (74 hrs; *(1,2)*; 1 per week). Note: vessels also serve Hamburg and Antwerpen, working on a two week cycle, one clockwise, the other anti-clockwise.

VESSELS

1	BRUARFOSS	*13478t	78	17k	12P	–	144T	A	Kiel, GE	IC
2	LAXFOSS	*12817t	78	15.5k	12P	–	144T	A	Kiel, GE	IC

BRUARFOSS Built as the MERZARIO PERSIA for *Merzario Line* of Italy and used on services between Italy and the Middle East. In 1986 she was chartered to *Grimaldi Line* of Italy and renamed the PERSIA, continuing on Middle East services. In 1988 she was sold to *Eimskip* and renamed the BRUARFOSS.

LAXFOSS Built as the MERZARIO ARABIA for *Merzario Line* of Italy and used on services between Italy and the Middle East. In 1986 she was chartered to *Ignazio Messina* of Italy and renamed the JOLLY OCRA, continuing on Middle East services. In 1987, she was chartered to *Lloyd Triestino Line* of Italy and renamed the DUINO. In 1988 she was sold to *Eimskip* and renamed the LAXFOSS.

EUROAFRICA SHIPPING LINE

THE COMPANY *Euroafrica Shipping Line* is a Polish private sector company.

MANAGEMENT Managing Director: W Matuszewski, Deputy Managing Director: Z Ligierko.

ADDRESS *Poland:* Energetykow 3/4, 70952, Szczecin, Poland. *UK:* Gdynia-America Shipping, 238 City Road, LONDON EC1V 2QL.

TELEPHONE Administration & Reservations: *Poland:* +48 (0)91 334806. *UK:* +44 (0)71-253 9561, Fax: *Poland:* +48 (0)91 339183 & 337140, *UK:* +44 (0)71-250 3625, Telex: *Poland:* 422387 & 422396. *UK:* 23256.

ROUTE OPERATED Gdynia – Tilbury – Middlesbrough (3/4 days; *(1)*; weekly). Note: triangular service, operating in a clockwise direction.

VESSEL

INOWROCLAW	6408t	80	15k	12P	–	116T	A	Rauma, FI	PO

INOWROCLAW Built for *Polish Ocean Lines*, previously a state owned company. Now chartered to *Euroafrica Shipping Line*.

FINANGLIA FERRIES

THE COMPANY *Finanglia Ferries* is a joint operation between *Finncarriers Oy Ab*, a Finnish private sector company and *United Baltic Corporation*, a British private sector company.

MANAGEMENT Managing Director: J Ashley, **Marketing Manager:** Miss C M Cotton.

ADDRESSES *UK:* Maritime House, 18 Ensign Street, LONDON E1 8JD, *Finland:* Porkkalankatu 7, 00181 Helsinki, Finland.

TELEPHONE Reservations and Administration: *UK:* +44 (0)71-481 0606, *Finland:* +358 (0) 134311, **Fax:** *UK:* +44 (0)71-488 4450, *Finland:* +358 (0) 13431200, **Telex:** *UK:* 887002, *Finland:* 1001743.

ROUTES OPERATED Felixstowe – Helsinki (Finland) – Hamina (Finland) (4 days; 2 per week northbound, 3 per week southbound), Hull – Helsinki – Hamina (5 days; 1 per week). Note: Finland – Hull service operates via Felixstowe on southward journey giving additional southward sailing. Vessels operate on weekly, two and three weekly cycles and are frequently moved between routes.

VESSELS

1	AHLERS BALTIC	*21224t	90	19k	0P	–	182T	A	Ulsan, SK	CY
2	BALTIC EIDER	*20865	89	19k	0P	–	180T	A	Ulsan, SK	IM
3	BORE BRITANNICA	5761t	78	17K	0P	–	174T	A	Ulsan, SK	FI
4	BORE GOTHICA	5766t	78	17k	0P	–	174T	A	Ulsan, SK	SW
5	CELIA	9335t	79	16.5k	0P	–	136T	Q	Ichihara, JA	SW
6	CORTIA	9299t	78	19k	0P	–	136T	Q	Ichihara, JA	SW

AHLERS BALTIC Built for *Ahlers Line* and chartered to *Finncarriers*.

BALTIC EIDER Built for *United Baltic Corporation*.

BORE BRITANNICA Built as the ATLANTIC PROJECT for *Stena Line* and chartered to *ACL* of Great Britain for service between Britain and Canada. In 1981 chartered to *Merzario Line* of Italy for services between Italy and Saudi Arabia and renamed the MERZARIO HISPANIA. In 1983 returned to *Stena Line* and renamed the STENA HISPANIA. In 1984 chartered to *Kotka Line* of Finland, renamed the KOTKA VIOLET and used on their services between Finland, UK and West Africa. This charter ended in 1985 and she was again named the STENA HISPANIA. In 1986 she was renamed the STENA BRITANNICA and used on *Stena Portlink* (later *Stena Tor Line*) service between Sweden and Britain. In 1988 she was chartered to *Bore Line* of Finland, renamed the BORE BRITANNICA and used on services between Finland and Britain. In 1992 chartered to *Finncarriers*.

BORE GOTHICA Built as the ATLANTIC PROSPER for *Stena Line* and chartered *ACL* (see above). In 1981 chartered to *Merzario Line* of Italy for services between Italy and Saudi Arabia and renamed, initially, the STENA IONIA and then the MERZARIO IONIA. Later the same year she reverted to the name STENA IONIA and was chartered to *OT West Africa Line* for services between Europe and Nigeria. In 1985 she was renamed the STENA GOTHICA and used on *Stena Portlink* services. In 1988 she was chartered to *Bore Line* of Finland and renamed the BORE BRITANNICA. In 1992 chartered to *Finncarriers*.

CELIA Built as the VASALAND for *Boström AB* of Sweden and chartered to *EFFOA* of Finland for services between Scandinavia and Mediterranean ports. In 1984 chartered to *Swedish Orient Line* for similar services and renamed the HESPERUS. In 1986 sold to *Finncarriers* and renamed the CELIA.

CORTIA Built as the TIMMERLAND for *Boström AB* of Sweden and chartered to *EFFOA* of Finland for services between Scandinavia and Mediterranean ports. In 1984 chartered to *Swedish Orient Line* for similar services and renamed the HEKTOS. In 1986 sold to *Finncarriers* and renamed the CORTIA.

FRED. OLSEN LINES

THE COMPANY *Fred. Olsen Lines* is a Norwegian private sector company.

MANAGEMENT Marketing Manager: Tor Erik Andreassen.

ADDRESS Fred. Olsen Gate 2, PO Box 1159, Centrum, Oslo 1, Norway.

TELEPHONE Administration & Reservations: +47 22 34 10 00, **Fax:** . +47 22 41 24 15, **Telex:** 412415.

ROUTES OPERATED Oslo/East Norway – Immingham (2 per week), Oslo/East Norway – Felixstowe (1 per week). Vessels listed below also operate from Oslo and East Norway to Rotterdam, Hamburg and Zeebrugge. Vessels used on all services.

VESSELS

1	BALDUIN	5171t	75	18k	12P	–	142T	A	Florø, NO	NO
2	BORAC	8160t	78	18.5k	0P	–	208T	A	Oskarshamn, SW	NO
3	BORACAY	7825t	78	18k	0P	–	208T	A	Oskarshamn, SW	NO

BALDUIN Built for *Fred. Olsen Lines* for North Sea services.

BORAC Built as the EMIRATES EXPRESS for *A/S Skarhamns Oljetransport* of Norway and chartered to *Mideastcargo* for services between Europe and the Middle East. In 1981 chartered to *OT West Africa Line* for services between Europe and West Africa and renamed the ABUJA EXPRESS. In 1983 chartered to *Foss Line*, renamed the FOSSEAGLE and returned to Middle East service. In 1985 she was renamed the FINNEAGLE, chartered briefly to *Finncarriers* and then to *Fred. Olsen Lines*, who used her on UK – Norway services. In 1987 they purchased her and renamed her the BORAC.

BORACAY Built as the BANDAR ABBAS EXPRESS for *A/S Skarhamns Oljetransport* of Norway and chartered out. In 1980 renamed the SAUDI EXPRESS. During the early eighties she undertook a number of charters including *Mideastcargo* for services between Europe and the Middle East, *Atlanticargo* for services from Europe to USA and Mexico and *OT West Africa Line* (see above). In 1983 chartered to *Ignazio Messina* of Italy, renamed the JOLLY AVORIO and used on services from Italy to the Middle East. In 1986 this charter ended and she briefly reverted to the name the SAUDI EXPRESS before being chartered to *OT West Africa Line* and renamed the KARAWA. In 1987 she was sold to *Fred. Olsen Lines* who renamed her the BORACAY.

Merchant Bravery (Miles Cowsill)

Peveril (Miles Cowsill)

ISLE OF MAN STEAM PACKET COMPANY

THE COMPANY, MANAGEMENT, ADDRESS AND TELEPHONE See Section 1.

ROUTE OPERATED Douglas (Isle of Man) – Heysham (3 hrs 35 mins; *(1)*; daily).

VESSELS

1	PEVERIL	1976t	71	17k	12P	–	40T	A	Kristiansand, NO	GB

PEVERIL Built as the HOLMIA for *Rederi AB Silja* of Finland. She was used on *Silja Line* cargo and RO/RO services between Norrtälje (Sweden) and Turku (Finland). In 1973 she was sold and renamed the A S D METEOR. Later that year she was sold to *P&O Ferries* for their joint Heysham – Belfast service with *Sealink* and renamed the PENDA. In 1980 she was renamed the N F JAGUAR and transferred to freight services between Southampton and Le Havre. In 1981 she was chartered to *IOMSP* for a Liverpool – Heysham freight service and in 1983 she was demise chartered by *James Fisher* of Barrow and chartered to *IOMSP*. She was renamed the PEVERIL. The freight service was switched to Heysham in 1985. The charter ended in December 1992 and she was purchased by the *IOMSP*.

MANNIN LINE

THE COMPANY *Mannin Line* is a British private sector company, owned by the *Isle of Man Steam Packet Company* of the Isle of Man.

MANAGEMENT General Manager: Colin Crawford.

ADDRESS Atlas House, Southgate Road, GREAT YARMOUTH, Norfolk NR30 3LN.

TELEPHONE Administration: +44 (0)493 330000, Reservations: +44 (0)493 330000, Fax: +44 (0)493 330106.

ROUTE OPERATED Great Yarmouth – Ijmuiden (Netherlands) (8 hrs; *(1)*; daily).

VESSEL

BELARD	1599t	79	15.5k	0P	–	54T	AS	Frederikshavn, DK	GB

BELARD Built as the MERCANDIAN CARRIER II for *Mercandia* of Denmark and used on a variety of services. In 1983 she was briefly renamed ALIANZA and between 1984 and 1985 she carried the name CARRIER II. In 1985 sold to *P&O*, renamed the BELARD and used on *Northern Ireland Trailers* services between Ardrossan and Larne, subsequently marketed as part of *Pandoro*. In 1993 she was chartered to *Mannin Line* to inaugurate a new service between Great Yarmouth and Ijmuiden.

MERCHANT FERRIES

THE COMPANY *Merchant Ferries* is a British private sector company.

MANAGEMENT General Manager: Richard Harrison, Marketing Manager: Alistair Eagles.

ADDRESS North Quay, Heysham Harbour, MORCAMBE, Lancs LA3 2UL.

TELEPHONE Administration: +44 (0)524 855018, **Reservations:** +44 (0)524 855018, **Fax:** +44 (0)524 852527, **Telex:** 65445.

ROUTE OPERATED Heysham – Warrenpoint (8 hrs; *(1,2,3)*; 3 per day).

VESSELS

1	MERCHANT BRAVERY	*9368t	78	17k	12P	–	106T	A	Oslo, NO	BA
2	MERCHANT BRILLIANT	*9368t	79	17k	12P	–	106T	A	Kyrksæterøra, NO	BA
3	MERCHANT VENTURE	2955t	79	17k	12P	–	55T	A	Castelo, PL	IM

MERCHANT BRAVERY Launched as the STEVI for *Steineger & Wiik* of Norway and, on delivery, chartered to *Norient Line* of Norway, being renamed the NORWEGIAN CRUSADER. In 1980 chartered to *Ignazio Messina* of Italy for Mediterranean service and renamed the JOLLY GIALLO. In 1982 the charter ended and she was briefly renamed the NORWEGIAN CRUSADER before being purchased by *Ignazio Messina* and resuming the name JOLLY GIALLO. In 1993 sold to *Merchant Ferries*, renamed the MERCHANT BRAVERY and placed on the Heysham – Warrenpoint service.

MERCHANT BRILLIANT Built as the NORWEGIAN CHALLENGER for *Steineger & Wiik* of Norway and chartered to *Norient Line* of Norway. In 1982, chartered to *Ignazio Messina* of Italy for Mediterranean service and renamed the JOLLY BRUNO. Later in 1982 she was purchased by *Ignazio Messina*. In 1993 sold to *Merchant Ferries*, renamed the MERCHANT BRILLIANT and placed on the Heysham – Warrenpoint service.

MERCHANT VENTURE Built as the FARMAN and chartered to *GNMTC* of Italy for Mediterranean services. In 1982 she was sold to *Medlines* for similar service and renamed the MED ADRIATICO. In 1985 she was sold, renamed the ARGENTEA and chartered to *SGMAT*, continuing to operate in the Mediterranean. In 1987 sold to *Cenargo* and chartered to *Merchant Ferries* who renamed her first the MERCHANT ISLE and then the MERCHANT VENTURE. Until 1993 she was used on the Fleetwood – Warrenpoint service; in 1993 the Fleetwood service was switched to Heysham and she currently operates between Heysham and Warrenpoint.

MERIDIAN FERRIES

THE COMPANY *Meridian Ferries* is a British private sector company.

MANAGEMENT General Manager Paul Desgris, **Folkestone Manager:** Kevin Root.

ADDRESS Folkestone Harbour, FOLKESTONE, Kent CT20 1QH.

TELEPHONE Administration: +44 (0)303 220577, **Reservations:** +44 (0)303 220577. **Fax:** +44 (0)303 221789, **Telex:** 965543.

ROUTE OPERATED Folkestone – Boulogne (2 hrs 15 mins; *(1)*; 3 per day).

VESSEL

SPIRIT OF BOULOGNE	2794t	74	14.5k	50P	–	48T	A	Kristiansand, NO	BA

SPIRIT OF BOULOGNE Built for *A/S Larvik-Frederikshavnferjen* of Norway as DUKE OF YORKSHIRE. In 1978 she was chartered to (and later purchased by) *CN Marine* of Canada (from 1986 *Marine Atlantic*) and renamed the MARINE EVANGELINE. She was used on services between Canada, USA and Newfoundland. In 1992 she was chartered to *Opale Ferries* of France and inaugurated a new Boulogne – Folkestone freight service. In 1993 the company went into liquidation and the service and charter were taken over by *Meridian Ferries*, a British company. She was renamed the SPIRIT OF BOULOGNE.

NORCARGO

THE COMPANY *NorCargo* is a Norwegian Company jointly owned by *Det Bergenske DS (Bergen Line)* and *Det Nordenfjeldske DS.*

ADDRESS Dokkes Kjaerskainen, PO Box 2677, Moehlenpris, 5026 BERGEN, Norway.

TELEPHONE Administration & Bookings: *Bergen:* +47 55 32 00 00, *UK* +44 (0)472 240241, **Fax:** *Bergen:* +47 55 32 15 88, *UK:* +44 (0)472 240250.

ROUTES OPERATED Bergen, Stavanger, Sandnes, Harvik – Newcastle (1-3 days; *(1)*; weekly).

VESSEL

COMETA	1999t	81	16k	0P	–	28T	AS	Fosen, NO	NO

COMETA Built for *Nor-Cargo.*

NORFOLK LINE

THE COMPANY *Norfolk Line* is a Dutch private sector company owned by *A P Møler Finance* of Switzerland.

MANAGEMENT Managing Director: B E Hansen, **Marketing Manager:** R A Meijer, **General Manager UK:** E J Green.

ADDRESS *Netherlands:* Kranenburgweg 211, 2583 ER Scheveningen, Netherlands. *UK:* Norfolk House, The Dock, FELIXSTOWE, Suffolk IP11 8UY.

TELEPHONE Administration: *Netherlands:* +31 (0)70 352 74 00, *UK:* +44 (0)394 673676, **Reservations:** *Netherlands:* +31 (0)70 352 74 71, *Felixstowe:* +44 (0)394 603630, *North Shields:* +44 (0)91-296 1036, *Grimsby:* +44 (0)469 571122. **Fax (admin):** *Netherlands:* +31 (0)70 354 93 30, *UK:* +44 (0)394 603676. **Telex:** *Netherlands:* 31515. *UK:* 987698.

ROUTES OPERATED Felixstowe – Scheveningen (8 hrs; *(1,2)*; 2 per day), North Shields – Esbjerg (23 hrs; 2 per week), Grimsby – Esbjerg (22 hrs; 4 per week), Harwich – Esbjerg (21 hrs; 6 per week). Danish services marketed as *Brit Line* and operated in conjunction with *DFDS*; all vessels are provided by *DFDS*.

VESSELS

1	MAERSK FLANDERS	2574t	78	16k	12P	–	80T	A	Tokyo, JA	NL
2	ROSEANNE	2720t	82	17k	12P	–	78T	AS	Vigo, SP	CY

Norbank (North Sea Ferries)

Norland and European Pathway (John Hendy)

MAERSK FLANDERS Built as the ADMIRAL ATLANTIC for *Admiral Shipping* of the USA for Caribbean service. In 1983 she was chartered to *Portlink* for North Sea services. In 1984 sold to Swedish interests and renamed the ROMIRA. In 1986 she was sold to *Norfolk Line*, renamed the DUKE OF FLANDERS and used on their *Britline* services between Great Yarmouth and Esbjerg (Denmark). In 1990 she was renamed MAERSK FLANDERS. She now operates on the Felixstowe – Scheveningen route.

ROSEANNE Built as the REINA DEL CANTABRICO for *Labiad Andalusia* of Spain and chartered to *Matina Line* for services between Europe and West Africa. In 1983 renamed the SALAH LABIAD but resumed her original name in 1985. In 1987 she was sold, renamed FAROY and chartered to *Elbe-Humber Roline* for their service between Immingham and Cuxhaven. In 1989 sold again and renamed ROSEANNE; she was chartered to *P&O European Ferries* and used on their Felixstowe – Zeebrugge service. In 1991 chartered to *Norfolk Line*.

NORTH SEA FERRIES

THE COMPANY, MANAGEMENT, ADDRESS AND TELEPHONE See Section 1.

ROUTES OPERATED Hull – Rotterdam (Europoort) (10 hrs; *(2,3)*; daily), Middlesbrough – Zeebrugge (16 hrs; *(5,6)*; daily), Ipswich – Rotterdam (Europoort) (7 hrs 30 mins; *(4,7)*; 2 per day), Hull – Zeebrugge (16 hours; *(1,8)*; daily).

VESSELS

1	CAP CANAILLE	1576t	77	15k	12P	–	56T	A	Le Havre, FR	FR
2	NORBANK	*17464t	93	22k	114P	–	156T	A	Rotterdam, NL	NL
3	NORBAY	*17464	94	22k	114P	–	156T	BA	Rotterdam, NL	GB
4	NORCAPE	6310t	79	18.7k	12P	–	138T	A	Tamano, JA	NL
5	NORKING	6850t	80	17.5K	12P	–	130T	A	Rauma, FI	FI
6	NORQUEEN	6849t	80	17.5K	12P	–	130T	A	Rauma, FI	FI
5	NORSKY	6310t	79	18.0k	12P	–	138T	A	Tamano, JA	GB
8	SALLY EUROBRIDGE	1599t	77	16k	12P	–	70T	A	Bremerhaven, GE	BA

CAP CANAILLE Built as the CAP LARDIER for *Chargeurs Réunis* of France for service between France and North Africa. In 1983, sold to *Société Daher* of France and renamed the GYPTIS, continuing to sail between France and Tunisia. In 1988 chartered to *VASCO* to operate between Britain and Spain; she was renamed the SEA FOWL. Other charters followed and in 1992 she was sold to *Conade* and renamed the LIBECCIO. Later that year she was renamed the CAP CANAILLE. In 1994 she was chartered to *North Sea Ferries* to operate between Hull and Zeebrugge.

NORBANK, NORBAY Built for *North Sea Ferries* for the Hull – Rotterdam freight service.

NORCAPE Launched as the PUMA but, on completion chartered to *B&I Line* and renamed the TIPPERARY for their Dublin – Liverpool service. In 1989 sold to *North Sea Ferries*, renamed the NORCAPE and introduced onto the Ipswich – Rotterdam service.

NORKING, NORQUEEN Built as the BORE KING and the BORE QUEEN for *Bore Line* of Finland for Baltic services. In 1991 chartered to *North Sea Ferries* for their Middlesbrough – Zeebrugge service and renamed the NORKING and NORQUEEN respectively.

NORSKY Built as the IBEX for *P&O (Pandoro)* for their Irish sea services. In 1980 transferred to *North Sea*

Ferries, renamed the NORSEA and used on the Ipswich – Rotterdam service. In 1986 she was renamed the NORSKY.

SALLY EUROBRIDGE Built as the MASHALA for *Mashala Shipping* of Italy and chartered to *Gilnavi* for Mediterranean services. After a long period out of service in the mid-nineteen eighties, in 1987 she was sold, renamed the HALLA and chartered for Caribbean service. In 1988 she was renamed the TIKAL. In 1989 she was sold to *Schiaffino Line* of France, renamed the SCHIAFFINO and put into service between Ramsgate and Oostende. In 1990 the company was taken over by *Sally Ferries* and in 1991 she was chartered to *Belfast Freight Ferries*. In 1993 she was renamed the SALLY EUROBRIDGE. In January 1994, chartered to *North Sea Ferries* to operate between Hull and Zeebrugge.

P&O EUROPEAN FERRIES

THE COMPANY See Section 1.

MANAGEMENT Freight Director (Dover): Brian Cork, **Freight Director (Portsmouth):** Lawrence Strover.

TELEPHONE Administration: See Section 1, **Reservations (freight):** *Dover:* 0304 223344, *Felixstowe:* +44 (0)394 604100, *Portsmouth:* +44 (0)705 772070, *Cairnryan:* +44 (0)581 200633/4/5, *Larne:* +44 (0)574 272201, **Fax:** *Dover:* 0304 223399, *Felixstowe:* +44 (0)394 604329, *Portsmouth:* +44 (0)705 772075, *Cairnryan:* +44 (0)581 200282, *Larne:* +44 (0)574 272477, **Telex:** *Dover:* 96316, *Felixstowe:* 98236, *Portsmouth:* 86806, *Cairnryan:* 779238, *Larne:* 74528.

ROUTES OPERATED Portsmouth – Le Havre (5 hrs 30 mins; *(7,8)*; daily); 2 per day), Dover – Zeebrugge (4 hrs; *(1,3,4,5)*; 6 per day). Felixstowe – Rotterdam (Europoort) (7 hrs 30 mins; *(2,6)*; 2 per day).

VESSELS

1	EUROPEAN ENDEAVOUR	3367t	78	17.5k	107P	–	46T	BA2	Bremerhaven, GE	GB
2	EUROPEAN FREEWAY	8579t	77	17k	166P	–	163T	A2	Ulsan, SK	GB
3	EUROPEAN HIGHWAY	*22986t	92	21k	200P	–	120T	BA2	Bremerhaven, GE	GB
4	EUROPEAN PATHWAY	*22986t	92	21k	200P	–	120T	BA2	Bremerhaven, GE	GB
5	EUROPEAN SEAWAY	*22986t	91	21k	200P	–	120T	BA2	Bremerhaven, GE	GB
6	EUROPEAN TIDEWAY	8583t	77	17k	166P	–	163T	A2	Ulsan, SK	GB
7	EUROPEAN TRADER	3367t	75	17.5k	107P	–	46T	BA2	Bremerhaven, GE	GB
8	GABRIELE WEHR	2185t	78	15k	12P	–	80T	A	Hamburg, GE	GE

EUROPEAN ENDEAVOUR, EUROPEAN TRADER Built for *European Ferries* RO/RO freight services. The EUROPEAN TRADER was built to a standard design rather than custom built. The EUROPEAN ENDEAVOUR was originally named EUROPEAN ENTERPRISE and renamed in 1988. They were all used on freight services between Dover and Calais and Dover and Zeebrugge. If space was available, a small number of passengers was sometimes conveyed on the Zeebrugge service, although the sailings were not advertised for passengers. This ceased with the withdrawal of passenger services on this route at the end of 1991. In late 1991, the EUROPEAN TRADER was transferred to the Portsmouth – Le Havre route. The EUROPEAN ENDEAVOUR remains on the Dover – Zeebrugge service but has also served as a replacement vessel on the Felixstowe – Rotterdam service and in 1994 at Larne.

EUROPEAN FREEWAY Built for *Stena Line* as the ALPHA ENTERPRISE and chartered to *Aghiris Navigation* of Cyprus. In 1979 she was renamed the SYRIA and chartered to *Hellas Ferries* for services between Greece and Syria. In 1981 she was lengthened by 33.6m. In 1982 she was chartered to *European Ferries* and used on freight services between Felixstowe and Europoort. In 1983 she was renamed the STENA TRANSPORTER and in 1986 the CERDIC FERRY. In 1992 she was renamed the EUROPEAN FREEWAY.

EUROPEAN HIGHWAY, EUROPEAN PATHWAY, EUROPEAN SEAWAY Built for *P&O European Ferries* for the Dover – Zeebrugge freight service.

EUROPEAN TIDEWAY Launched as the STENA RUNNER. On completion, renamed the ALPHA PROGRESS for *Aghiris Navigation* of Greece. In 1979 renamed the HELLAS and operated by *Hellas Ferries* on services between Greece and Syria. In 1982 she was lengthened by 33.6m. In 1982 she was chartered to *European Ferries* and used on freight services between Felixstowe and Rotterdam (Europoort). The following year she was returned to *Hellas Ferries*. In 1985 she returned to *European Ferries* and the Rotterdam service. In 1986 she was renamed the DORIC FERRY. In 1992 she was renamed the EUROPEAN TIDEWAY.

GABRIELE WEHR Built for *Wehr Transport* of Germany and chartered to several operators. In 1982, chartered to *Tor Lloyd* (later *Tor Line*) for North Sea service and renamed the TOR ANGLIA. This charter terminated in 1985 when she resumed her original name and, in early 1986, she was chartered to *North Sea Ferries* for their Hull – Zeebrugge service. This charter ended in summer 1987 when the lengthened NORLAND and NORSTAR entered service. Subsequent charters included *Kent Line* and *Brittany Ferries*. In 1989 she was chartered to *P&O European Ferries* for the Portsmouth – Le Havre freight service. The charter was terminated following the transfer of the EUROPEAN TRADER to the route in late 1992 but has been renewed following the transfer of the EUROPEAN CLEARWAY to *Pandoro*.

P&O FERRYMASTERS

THE COMPANY *P&O Ferrymasters Ltd* is a British private sector company, part of the *P&O Group*.

MANAGEMENT Managing Director: D Munt, Marketing Manager: G B Kendren.

ADDRESS Station House, Stamford New Road, ALTRINCHAM, Cheshire WA14 1ER.

TELEPHONE Administration: +44 (0)642 455591, Reservations: +44 (0)642 455591, Fax: +44 (0)642 453439, Telex: 587491.

ROUTE OPERATED Middlesbrough – Göteborg (Sweden) – Helsingborg (Sweden)(up to 48 hrs; *(1)*; 2 per week).

VESSEL

ELK	*14374t	78	18k	12P	–	140T	A	Ulsan, SK	GB

ELK Built for *P&O Ferrymasters*. Lengthened in 1986.

Normandie Shipper (Truckline)

P&O SCOTTISH FERRIES

THE COMPANY, MANAGEMENT AND ADDRESS See Section 1.

TELEPHONE Administration: +44 (0)224 589111, **Reservations:** +44 (0)224 589111, **Fax:** +44 (0)574411, **Telex:** 73344.

ROUTES OPERATED Aberdeen-Lerwick (14hrs; *(1)*; up to 4 per week) One southbound trip returns via Stromness or Kirkwall taking approx. 20 hours.

VESSEL

ST ROGNVALD	2645t	70	16.5k	26P	80C	38L	A	Lübeck, GE	GB

ST ROGNVALD Launched as the RHONETAL but renamed NORCAPE on delivery. She resumed the name RHONETAL in 1974. In 1975 sold to *Meridional D'Armements* of France for services to Corsica and renamed the RHONE. In 1987 sold to *Conadir* of Italy for Mediterranean services and renamed MARINO TORRE. In 1989 taken on six months charter to *P&O Scottish Ferries*. In 1990 she was purchased by them and renamed ST ROGNVALD. She initially operated alongside and then replaced the ST MAGNUS (1206t, 1970). Earlier calls at Leith, Hanstholm (Denmark) and Kristiansand (Norway) have now been discontinued.

PANDORO

THE COMPANY *Pandoro* is a British private sector company, part of the *P&O Group*.

MANAGEMENT Managing Director: A G B Crean, **Commercial Director:** Martin Taylor.

ADDRESS Dock Street, FLEETWOOD, Lancashire FY7 6HR.

TELEPHONE Administration & Reservations: +44 (0)253 777111, **Fax:** +44 (0)253 777111. **Telex:** 67166 PD FWD G.

ROUTES OPERATED Ardrossan – Larne (5 hrs; *(4)*; 1 per day), Fleetwood – Larne (7 hrs; *(5,6)*; 2 per day), Liverpool – Dublin (7 hrs; *(1,2)*; 2 per day), Cherbourg – Rosslare (17 hrs; *(4)*; 3 per week).

VESSELS

1	BISON	4259t	75	18.5k	76P	–	120T	A	Hamburg, GE	GB
2	BUFFALO	*10987t	75	18.5k	45P	–	120T	A	Hamburg, GE	FI
3	EUROPEAN CLEARWAY	3334t	75	19k	132P	–	76T	BA	Bremerhaven, GE	GB
4	MERCHANT VALIANT	1598t	78	16k	12P	–	71T	A	Bremerhaven, GE	BA
5	PUMA	4377t	75	18k	40P	–	100T	A	Bremerhaven, GE	GB
6	VIKING TRADER	3985t	77	18k	48P	–	92T	A	Korneuburg, AU	GB

BISON Built for *P&O*. Between 1989 and 1993 operated by *B&I Line* of Ireland on a joint service with *Pandoro*. Used on the Liverpool – Dublin service.

BUFFALO Built for *P&O*. Lengthened in 1988. Used on the Liverpool – Dublin service

EUROPEAN CLEARWAY Built for *European Ferries* RO/RO freight services. She was built to a standard design rather than custom built. She was used on freight services between Dover and Calais and Dover and Zeebrugge. In 1992 she was moved to the Portsmouth – Le Havre route. In 1993 she was transferred to *Pandoro* to inaugurate a new Cherbourg – Rosslare service.

MERCHANT VALIANT Built as the SALAHALA and chartered to *Gilnavi* of Italy for Mediterranean services. In 1990 she was purchased by *Cenargo* and chartered to *Merchant Ferries* who renamed her the MERCHANT VALIANT. She was used on the Fleetwood – Warrenpoint service until 1993 when she was chartered to *Pandoro* and placed on their Ardrossan – Larne service.

PUMA Built as the UNION TRADER for *Northern Coasters* of the Irish Republic. In 1980 briefly renamed the UNION MELBOURNE before being sold to *P&O* and renamed the PUMA. She is used on the Fleetwood – Larne service.

VIKING TRADER Launched as the STENA TRADER but entered service as the GOYA for *United Baltic Corporation* of Great Britain on services between Britain and Finland. In 1981 sold to *Federal Commerce* of Canada for Canadian service and renamed the FEDERAL NOVA. In 1981 briefly renamed the CARIBBEAN SKY before being sold to *Linea Manuare* of Venezuela and renamed the MANUARE VII and used on services to the USA. In 1983 sold and chartered to *Navigation Central* and renamed the OYSTER BAY. Later that year she was chartered to *European Ferries*, renamed the VIKING TRADER and used on services between Portsmouth and France. In 1989 transferred to *Pandoro*. Currently used on the Fleetwood – Larne service.

SALLY FERRIES

THE COMPANY, MANAGEMENT AND ADDRESS See Section 1.

TELEPHONE Administration: +44 (0)843 585151 **Reservations:** +44 (0)843 585151. **Fax:** +44 (0)843 580894. **Telex:** 96352.

ROUTES OPERATED Ramsgate – Dunkerque Ouest (2 hrs 30 mins; *(3)*; 2 per day), Ramsgate – Oostende (4 hrs 30 mins; *(1,2)*; 3 per day).

VESSELS

1	SALLY EUROLINK	*2831t	85	15k	0P	–	100T	A	Galatz, RO	BA
2	SALLY EUROROUTE	*2831t	85	15k	0P	–	100T	A	Galatz, RO	BA
3	SALLY SUN	1595t	79	16k	52P	–	66T	BA	Falkenburg, SW	IM

SALLY EUROLINK Launched as the BALDER BRE. On completion sold to *Navrom* of Romania and renamed the BAZIAS 4. In 1991 chartered to *Sally Ferries* for the Ramsgate – Oostende freight service. In 1993 renamed the SALLY EUROLINK and re-registered in The Bahamas.

SALLY EUROROUTE Launched as the BALDER STEN. On completion sold to *Navrom* of Romania and renamed the BAZIAS 3. In 1991 chartered to *Sally Ferries* for the Ramsgate – Oostende freight service. In 1993 renamed the SALLY EUROROUTE and re-registered in The Bahamas.

SALLY SUN Built as the GUTE for *Gotlandsbolaget* of Sweden for services between the Swedish mainland and the island of Gotland. In 1987 she was chartered to *Brambles Shipping* of Australia and in 1988 she was re-registered in the Isle of Man. In 1992 she was charted to *Sally Ferries*, renamed SALLY SUN and started freight only sailings on the Ramsgate – Dunkerque route.

Viking Trader (Miles Cowsill)

SEALINK – SNAT

THE COMPANY, MANAGEMENT, ADDRESS AND TELEPHONE See Section 1.

ROUTE OPERATED Dunkerque Ouest – Dover (train ferry) (2hrs 30 mins hrs; *(1)*; 2-3 per day).

VESSEL

NORD PAS-DE-CALAIS	*13727t	87	21.5k	80P	–	37R	BA2	Dunkerque, FR	FR

NORD PAS-DE-CALAIS Built for *SNCF* for the Dunkerque Ouest – Dover train ferry service to replace the SAINT ELOI (see the KING ORRY, *Isle of Man Steam Packet Company*) and SAINT-GERMAIN (3492t, 1951). Before being used on the train ferry service (which required the construction of a new berth at Dover (Western Docks)) in May 1988, she operated road freight services from Calais to Dover Eastern Docks. She will continue to operate following the opening of the Channel Tunnel in 1994 to convey dangerous loads which will be banned from the tunnel, although Railfreight Distribution do not see the operation carrying on after 1995.

STENA SEALINK LINE

THE COMPANY, MANAGEMENT, ADDRESS AND TELEPHONE See Section 1.

ROUTE OPERATED Dover – Dunkerque Ouest (2 hrs 30 mins; *(see below)*; up to 3 daily).

VESSEL

The STENA CHALLENGER (see Section 1) operates during the winter. During the summer period (May – September) this vessel will operate passenger sailings between Dover and Calais and is expected to be replaced by a chartered vessel. At the time of going to press details are not available.

Vessels may be chartered to supplement passenger ships on other routes during the summer period.

TOR LINE

THE COMPANY *Tor Line* is one of the trading names of the freight division of *DFDS A/S*, a Danish private sector company. See also *DFDS* (Danish services).

MANAGEMENT Managing Director UK: Ebbe Pederson.

ADDRESS Scandinavia House, Parkeston Quay, HARWICH CO12 4QG.

TELEPHONE Administration: +44 (0)255 242242, **Fax:** +44 (0)255 244310, **Telex:** 98582.

ROUTES OPERATED Harwich – Göteborg (24 hrs; 5 per week), Immingham – Göteborg (34 hrs; 5 per week), Immingham – Helsingborg (40 hrs; 1 per week). Note: Vessels are interwork on various *Tor Line* services between Sweden and Britain and other continental ports so it is not possible to assign vessels to specific services.

VESSELS

1	STENA GOTHICA	*14406t	75	18k	0P	–	150T	A	Sandefjord, NO	BA
2	TOR ANGLIA	13652t	77	17.5k	12P	–	196T	A	Kiel, GE	SW
3	TOR BRITANNIA	8690t	78	16k	12P	–	94T	AS	Dunkerque, FR	SW
4	TOR CALEDONIA	5983t	77	17k	12P	–	160T	A	Sandefjord, NO	DK
5	TOR FLANDRIA	*16947t	78	15k	12P	–	183T	A	Landskrona, SW	SW
6	TOR GOTHIA	5019t	71	17k	12P	–	120T	A	Sandefjord, NO	SW
7	TOR HOLLANDIA	5052t	73	17k	12P	–	120T	A	Sandefjord, NO	SW

STENA GOTHICA Built as the MELBOURNE TRADER for *Australian National Line* for services in Australia. In 1987 sold to *Forest Shipping* and then in 1988 sold to *Cotunav* and renamed the MONAWAR L. In 1990 she was sold to *Stena Line,* renamed the STENA GOTHICA, 'stretched' and chartered to *Tor Line*.

TOR ANGLIA Built as the MERZARIO GALLIA and chartered to *Merzario Line* of Italy for services between Italy and Saudi Arabia. In 1981 she was chartered to *Wilhelmsen,* renamed TANA and used between USA and West Africa. In 1983 she was chartered to *Salenia AB* of Sweden and renamed the NORDIC WASA. In 1987 she had a brief period on charter to *Atlantic Marine* as the AFRICAN GATEWAY and later that year she was chartered to *Tor Line* and renamed the TOR ANGLIA.

TOR BRITANNIA Built as the VILLE DU HAVRE for *Société Française de Transports Maritimes* of France. Between 1979 and 1981 she was renamed the FOSS HAVRE. In 1987 she was renamed the KAMINA. In 1990 she was chartered to *Maersk Line* of Denmark, renamed the MAERSK KENT and used on *Kent Line* services between Dartford and Zeebrugge. In 1992 she was chartered to and later purchased by *Tor Line* and renamed the TOR BRITANNIA.

TOR CALEDONIA Built for charter to *Tor Line* for freight service between Sweden and UK/Netherlands. In 1984 she was chartered to *Grimaldi Lines* of Italy, renamed the GOTHIC WASA. Later that year she was renamed the GALLOWAY but in 1985 she was returned to *Tor Line* and renamed the TOR CALEDONIA. In 1988 she was purchased.

TOR FLANDRIA Built as the ANNA ODEN for *Nordsjöfrakt* of Sweden. In 1981 chartered to *Tor Line*. In 1987 renamed the TOR FLANDRIA and in 1988 'stretched' in Flensburg, Germany.

TOR GOTHIA Built for *Tor Line*.

TOR HOLLANDIA Built for charter to *Tor Line*. In 1975 she was chartered to *Salenrederierna* for service in the Middle East and renamed the BANDAR ABBAS EXPRESS. In 1978 she was lengthened and returned to *Tor Line* and resumed the name TOR DANIA. Purchased by *Tor Line* in 1986. In 1992 she was renamed the TOR DAN and in 1993 the TOR HOLLANDIA.

TRUCKLINE FERRIES

THE COMPANY *Truckline Ferries* is *Brittany Ferries'* freight division.

MANAGEMENT Managing Director: Ian Carruthers, **Freight Director:** Gordon Day.

ADDRESS Truckline Ferries, New Harbour Road, POOLE, Dorset BH15 4AJ.

TELEPHONE Administration & Reservations: +44 (0)202 675048. **Fax:** +44 (0)202 679828. **Telex:** 41744, 41745.

ROUTES OPERATED Cherbourg – Poole (4 hrs 30 mins; *(1)*; 2 per day), Caen – Portsmouth (6 hrs; *(2)*; 1 per day).

VESSELS

| 1 | COUTANCES | *3046t | 78 | 17k | 58P | – | 64T | BA | Le Havre, FR | FR |
| 2 | NORMANDIE SHIPPER | 4078t | 73 | 17k | 36P | – | 86T | BA | Crepelle a/d Ijssel, NL | CI |

COUTANCES Built for *Truckline Ferries* for their Cherbourg – Poole service. In 1986 stretched to increase vehicle capacity by 34%.

NORMANDIE SHIPPER Built as the UNION WELLINGTON. In 1977 chartered to *Aghiris Navigation* of Greece and renamed the ALPHA EXPRESS. Later that year sold to *Stena Line*, renamed the STENA SHIPPER and used on a variety of services. In 1980 chartered to *Sealink*, rail tracks were fitted and she was operated on the Harwich – Zeebrugge train ferry service, being renamed the SPEEDLINK VANGUARD. In 1987 the charter was terminated, rail tracks were removed and, after a brief period as the CARIBE EXPRESS, she was renamed the STENA SHIPPER. In 1988 she was chartered to *Kirk Line* of the USA for service in the Caribbean and renamed the KIRK SHIPPER. In 1989 she was chartered to *Truckline Ferries*, renamed the NORMANDIE SHIPPER and inaugurated a Caen – Portsmouth freight service.

WASHBAY LINIE

THE COMPANY *Washbay Linie Gmbh* is a German private sector company.

MANAGEMENT Managing Director: Peter Stahl, **Marketing Manager:** H-E Toepfer.

ADDRESS (Raboisen 6), Postbox 10 60 60, D-20041, HAMBURG, Germany.

TELEPHONE Administration & Reservations: +49 (0)40 321 321, **Fax:** +49 (0)40-335 805, **Telex:** 216-1331.

ROUTES OPERATED Hamburg – King's Lynn (31 hrs; *(1)*; 2 per week), Hamburg – Grangemouth (42 hrs; *(2)*; 2 per week.

VESSELS

1	ALSTER RAPID	*3640t	86	13k	6P	480C	20T	A	Hamburg, GE	GE
2	HENRY STAHL	2332t	73	12k	4P	260C	15T	A	Emden, GE	GE

ALSTER RAPID, HENRY STAHL Built for *Washbay Line*. Both vessels are RO/LO freighters – ie they carry a combined cargo of wheeled traffic (including trade cars) and crane loaded containers.

SECTION 5 - OTHER VEHICLE FERRIES

In addition to the ferries listed above, there are a number of short chain ferries, cable ferries and ferries operated by unpowered floats:

Bournemouth-Swanage Motor Road and Ferry Company BRAMBLEBUSH BAY (1993) *(chain ferry)* **Route:** Sandbanks – Studland (Dorset).

C Toms & Son NO 3 (1963), NO 4 (1975) *(floats propelled by motor launches)*; **Route:** Fowey – Bodinnick (Cornwall).

Cumbria County Council MALLARD (1990) *(chain ferry)*; **Route:** Across Windermere (near Bowness-on-Windermere).

Isle of Wight County Council NO 5 (1976) *(chain ferry)*; **Route:** Cowes – East Cowes.

King Harry Steam Ferry Company KING HARRY FERRY (1974) *(chain ferry)*; **Route:** Across River Fal, King Harry Ferry (Cornwall).

Philip & Son DARTMOUTH/KINGSWEAR HIGHER FERRY (1960) *(diesel electric paddle propelled vessel guided by cross-river cable)*; **Route:** Dartmouth – Kingswear (Devon) across River Dart (higher route).

Reedham Ferry REEDHAM FERRY (1983) *(chain ferry)*; **Route:** Reedham – Norton (across River Yare, Norfolk).

South Hams District Council DARTMOUTH FERRY FLOAT II (1947), DARTMOUTH FERRY FLOAT III (1958) *(floats propelled by tugs)*; **Route:** Dartmouth – Kingswear (Devon) across River Dart (lower route).

Torpoint Ferry LYNHER (1961), PLYM (1968), TAMAR (1960) *(chain ferries)*; **Route:** Devonport (Devon) – Torpoint (Cornwall) across the Hamoaze.

Waterford Castle Hotel LITTLE ISLAND FERRY *(chain ferry)*; **Route:** Grantstown – Little Island (in River Suir, County Waterford).

MAJOR PASSENGER FERRY OPERATORS

There are a surprisingly large number of passenger only ferries operating in the British Isles, mainly operated by launches and small motor boats. There are, however, a few 'major' operators who operate only passenger vessels (of rather larger dimensions) and have not therefore been mentioned previously.

Clyde Marine Motoring FENCER (18t, 1976, 51 passengers), KENILWORTH (44t, 1936, 150 passengers), ROVER (48t, 1964, 120 passengers), THE SECOND SNARK (45t, 1938, 120 passengers). **Route Operated:** Gourock – Kilcreggan – Helensburgh.

Gosport Ferry GOSPORT QUEEN (159t, 1966, 550 passengers), PORTSMOUTH QUEEN (159t, 1966, 500 passengers), SOLENT ENTERPRISE (274t, 1971, 500 passengers (ex GAY ENTERPRISE)). **Route operated:** Gosport – Portsmouth.

Lundy Company OLDENBURG (288t, 1958, 267 passengers). **Routes Operated:** Bideford – Lundy Island, Ilfracombe – Lundy Island.

Mersey Ferries MOUNTWOOD (646t, 1960, 1118 passengers), OVERCHURCH (468t, 1962, 1200 passengers), WOODCHURCH (464t, 1960, 1102 passengers). **Routes operated:** Liverpool – Birkenhead (Woodside), Liverpool – Wallasey (Seacombe).

Tyne & Wear PTE PRIDE OF THE TYNE (222t, 1993, 350 passengers), SHIELDSMAN (93t, 1976, 350 passengers). **Route operated:** North Shields – South Shields.

White Horse Ferries GREAT EXPECTATIONS (66t, 1992, 95 passengers)(catamaran). **Route operated:** Gravesend (Kent) – Tilbury (Essex). HOTSPUR IV (50t, 1946, 243 passengers), HYTHE HOTSPUR (119t, 1974, 150 passengers), NEW FORESTER (49t, 1982, 97 passengers). **Route operated:** Southampton – Hythe (Hants). A high speed vessel is planned.

FAREWELL TO...

The following vessels, listed in 'Car Ferries of the British Isles 1992/93 and the 1993 Supplement have been disposed of – either to other companies listed in this book or others. Also listed are vessels which are no longer listed because they have ceased to serve ports in the British Isles. Company names are as used in that publication.

ARMORIQUE *(Brittany Ferries)* Sold in 1993 to the *Government of China.*

BEAUPORT *(British Channel Island Ferries)* The charter terminated at the end of the 1993 summer season.

CELTIC PRIDE *(Swansea Cork Ferries)* Charter terminated at the end of 1992 summer season. She returned to *Polferries* for Baltic services and resumed the name ROGALIN.

CHARTRES *(Sealink – ALA)* At the end of the 1993 summer season, withdrawn and sold to *Agapitos Lines* of Greece and renamed the EXPRESS SANTORINI.

EUROPEAN CLEARWAY *(P&O European Ferries)* In 1993 transferred to *Pandoro* to inaugurate a new Rosslare – Cherbourg freight service.

HOVERSPEED BOULOGNE *(Hoverspeed)* In 1993 transferred to a new *Sea Containers* service between Göteborg (Sweden) and Frederikshavn (Denmark) and renamed firstly the SEACAT DANMARK and then the SEACATAMARAN DENMARK.

IONIC FERRY *(P&O European Ferries)* Withdrawn in 1992, sold to Marlines of Greece and renamed the VISCOUNTESS M.

KEPPEL *(Caledonian MacBrayne)* In 1992 sold to *Inverclyde Marine* and renamed CLYDE ROSE.

KILBRANNAN *(Caledonian MacBrayne)* In 1992 sold to *Maoin-na-Farraige* of the Irish Republic and renamed the ÁRAINN MHOR.

MISNACH *(Maoin-na-Farraige)* In 1992 sold to *Bere Island Ferries*. Not renamed.

NORCLIFF *(North Sea Ferries)* Charter terminated in autumn 1993. Returned to *DSR Line* and resumed the name FICHTELBURG (not AUERSBERG as stated in supplement). In 1994 chartered to *DFDS*.

NORCREST *(North Sea Ferries)* Charter terminated in autumn 1992. Resumed original name, the WESERTAL.

NORCOVE *(North Sea Ferries)* Charter terminated 1994.

NORRÖNA *(Smyril Line)* This vessel no longer serves ports in the British Isles.

OLAU BRITANNIA, OLAU HOLLANDIA *(Olau Line)* In 1994 transferred to *TT Line* to operate between Travemünde and Trelleborg. Renamed the NILS HOLGERSSON and the PETER PAN>

PRIDE OF CANTERBURY *(P&O European Ferries)* Following the cessation of the Dover – Boulogne service in 1993, sold to *G A Ferries* of Greece and renamed the ROMILDA.

PRIDE OF HYTHE *(P&O European Ferries)* Following the cessation of the Dover – Boulogne service in 1993, sold to Greek interests and renamed the LABURNUM.

STENA BRITANNICA *(Stena Line)* In 1994 transferred to the Goteborg - Oslo service and renamed the STENA SAGA

STENA TRAVELLER *(Sealink Stena Line)* At the end of the 1992 summer season, charter transferred to *TT Line* of Germany and renamed the TT TRAVELLER.

SURREY *(Scandinavian Seaways)* In 1992 sold to Greek buyers and renamed the PATRA.

TRONDENES *(Island Ferries (CI))* The service has ceased following the liquidation of the company. The TRONDENES is for sale.

Sally Eurolink, as the **Bazias** 4 (John Hendy)

VESSELS RENAMED

The following vessels, listed in 'Car Ferries of the British Isles 1992/93' and the 1993 Supplement have been renamed, although they have not changed hands (other than by take over of one company by another). Company names are as used in that publication.

BAZIAS 3 *(Sally Ferries)* In 1993 renamed the SALLY EUROROUTE.
BAZIAS 4 *(Sally Ferries)* In 1993 renamed the SALLY EUROLINK.
HOVERSPEED FRANCE *(Hoverspeed)* In 1993 renamed the SEACAT BOULOGNE.
LEINSTER *(B&I Line)* In 1993 renamed the ISLE OF INISHMORE.
NILS HOLGERSSON *(Brittany Ferries)* In 1993 renamed the VAL DE LOIRE.
SEACAT TASMANIA *(Hoverspeed)* In 1993 renamed the SEACAT CALAIS.
TOR DANIA *(Tor Line)* In 1992 renamed the TOR DAN in preparation for sale. However, she was retained and in 1993 renamed the TOR HOLLANDIA.

NAMES OF SHIPS

NOTE: Only those ferries with names whose derivation is not immediately obvious are shown. Thus vessels named after everyday things, ports or islands served by the company's ferries and contrived names like NORLAND or OLAU HOLLANDIA are not listed.

ALSTER RAPID The Alster is a lake in the middle of Hamburg.
ARANN MHOR Gaelic name for Arranmore.
BELARD Combination of Belfast and Ardrossan ports.
BALTIC EIDER An eider is a species of duck.
BARFLEUR Village on North East corner of Cotentin peninsula.
BELNAHUA Small uninhabited island, about 1.2 miles off Luing.
BELAVUX Village in south east Belgium.
BIGGA Small, uninhabited island in Yell Sound, Shetland.
BRETAGNE French for Brittany.
BRUARFOSS Icelandic waterfall.
BRUERNISH Hamlet and peninsula on the island of Barra.
CAEDMON English poet who died c680 AD. Author of 'The Anglo Saxon Chronicle'.
CANNA Small Inner Hebridean Island.
CENRED Anglo Saxon King of Wessex.
CENWULF Tenth Century Bishop of Winchester. Died 1006.
CLAYMORE Double-edged broadsword used by Scottish Highlanders.
COLL Inner Hebridean Island.
COTE D'AZUR Literally 'Blue Coast'. Portion of French Mediterranean coast between Isles d'Hyres and the Italian frontier.
COUTANCES Town 41 miles south of Cherbourg
COWES CASTLE Castle on north coast of Isle of Wight, north of the town of Cowes. Home of the Royal Yacht Squadron.
CYMBELINE Fictitious king of Britain; subject of Shakespeare play.

DANA CIMBRIA The Cimbri were a Germanic tribe from North Jutland, who battled with the Romans but were finally defeated in 101BC.

DANA MAXIMA The maximum sized vessel that could use the port of Grimsby at the time she was introduced.

DUC DE NORMANDIE William Duke of Normandy, c1027-1087. He defeated King Harold II in 1066 and seized the English throne, becoming King William I.

DUCHESSE ANNE (1477-1514) Duchess of Brittany 1488-1514. Her marriages to King Charles VII of France and his successor Louis XII initiated the union of Brittany with France, despite Anne's desire to preserve Breton autonomy.

EARL SIGURD Viking ruler of Orkney during the 'Dark Ages'.

EARL THORFINN Viking ruler of Orkney during the 'Dark Ages'.

EGLANTINE Type of wild rose; also known as 'Sweet Briar'.

EIGG Small Inner Hebridean island.

EILEAN BEHEARNARAIGH Gaelic for 'Island of Berneray'.

EILEAN NA H-OIGE Gaelic for 'Island of Eriskay'.

EMERAUDE French for 'emerald'. The coastline between Cap Fréel and Pointe du Grouin is known as the 'Côte d'Emeraude' (Emerald Coast).

ERNEST BEVIN Labour politician and trade union leader 1881-1951. Minister in wartime coalition and postwar Labour Government. Latterly MP for Woolwich.

EYNHALLOW One of the Orkney Islands (small island between Mainland and Fousay).

F.B.D DUNBRODY 'F.B.D' stands for 'Farm Business Development', an agency of the Irish Farmers Association, which provided funding for the ferry service. 'Dunbrody' is a Cistercian Abbey in County Wexford, overlooking Waterford Harbour. Dissolved in the sixteenth century it is now a ruin.

FICHTELBERG Mountain in southern part of Germany.

FILLA Small, uninhabited island, part of Out Skerries, Shetland.

FIVLA Norwegian girl's name.

FYLGA Norwegian girl's name.

GEIRA Norwegian girl's name.

GLENACHULISH Glen leading east from Ballachulish.

GOOD SHEPHERD IV Traditional name for Fair Isle ferry. The term refers to Jesus Christ who is called thus several times in the Bible (eg John 10: verse 14).

GRIMA Norwegian girl's name.

GRY MARITHA Norwegian girl's name. Daughter of the vessel's original captain.

HAVELET Bay on which St Peter Port, Guernsey stands.

HENDRA Named after Henry Stewart, councillor for the Island of Whalsay, Shetland and clerk to the Community Council, who was instrumental in the acquisition of the vessel. In the local dialect, Henry is pronounced 'Hendry' and the name was then modified to fit in with the 'A' endings of the rest of the fleet.

HOY HEAD The derivation of this name – which is a traditional one – is unclear. Hoy is one of the Orkney Islands but there is no 'Hoy Head' as such on the island or on any other of the islands.

INOWROCLAW Town in central Poland.

IONA Small island off west coast of Mull.

ISLE OF INNISFREE Small island in Loch Gill, County Sligo. Subject of famous poem by W B Yeats, "The Lake Isle of Innisfree".

ISLE OF INISHMORE Largest of the Aran Islands, in Galway Bay, of the West coast of Ireland.

JAMES NEWMAN Labour politician 1879-1955. Mayor of Woolwich 1923- 1925 and 1951-1952.

JOHN BURNS Politician 1859-1943. Became cabinet minister in the Liberal government in 1905. Also student of London's history and river.

JUNO A leading goddess of the Roman pantheon, wife of Jupiter. Also a minor planet between Mars and Jupiter.

JUPITER Leading god of the Roman pantheon. Also fifth and largest planet of the solar system.

KING ORRY Norse chief Godred Croven, who seized the island in the eleventh century, was known to the Manx by this name.

KJELLA The vessel's original name, probably a Norwegian girl's name (pronounced 'Shella'). As it was in line with the rest of the fleet, it was not changed.

KOADA A stack, or rocky islet in Housa Voe, where the pier is situated on Papa Stour, Shetland.

KONINGIN BEATRIX Queen of the Netherlands, born 1938. Succeeded to the Dutch throne upon the abdication of her mother, Juliana, in 1980.

LAXFOSS Icelandic waterfall.

LEIRNA Area around the ferry terminal on Bressay

LOCH BUIE Small loch on south side of Mull.

LOCH DUNVEGAN Loch in north west of Skye.

LOCH FYNE Major loch which separates the northern part of the Kintyre peninsula and the rest of Scotland.

LOCH LINNHE Loch north of Oban, with Fort William at its head.

LOCH RANZA Small Loch on north end of Arran.

LOCH RIDDON Loch in south of Cowal peninsula, north of island of Bute.

LOCH STRIVEN Loch in south of Cowal peninsula, north east of island of Bute.

LOCH TARBERT There is no 'Loch Tarbert' as such. There are lochs called 'West Loch Tarbert' and 'East Loch Tarbert' on the Island of Harris and the Kintyre peninsula, with a village called 'Tarbert' between the two lochs.

LOCHMOR There are several small lochs in Scotland of this name.

LOVERVAL Village in southern Belgium near Charleroi.

LYONESSE LADY In ancient Cornish,'Lyonesse' means 'Land of the Sun God' and was the Celtic name for the islands, which lie directly west of Lands End. At certain times, the sun sets directly into the islands when viewed from Lands End.

MAID OF GLENCOUL Loch Glencoul leads south east from Kylesku, where the vessel originally operated.

MISNEACH The Gaelic word for 'courage'.

MORVERN Part of Scottish mainland to north east of Mull.

Portsmouth Queen and Duc de Normandie (John Hendy)

Pride of Bruges (Miles Cowsill)

NETLEY CASTLE House on Eastern side of Solent, about 2 miles SE of Southampton.

NORD PAS-DE-CALAIS The 'région' in which Boulogne, Calais and Dunkerque are situated.

NORDBORG Town on the island of Als, southern Denmark.

NORRIS CASTLE House in North of Isle of Wight, north of East Cowes.

NORSE LAGAN The Lagan is the river which Belfast is situated on.

NORSE MERSEY The Mersey is the river Liverpool is situated on.

PEVERIL Castle in Derbyshire. The Earls of Derby once owned the Isle of Man.

PRIDE OF AILSA Ailsa Craig is a small, uninhabited island about 10 miles from Galloway coast, almost due north of Cairnryan.

PRIDE OF BRUGES Bruges (known locally by its Flemish name 'Brugge') is a major town about 9 miles south of Zeebrugge.

PRIDE OF BURGUNDY Burgundy is a region of France, east of the Rhône and Saône.

PRIDE OF HAMPSHIRE Hampshire is the county in which Portsmouth is situated.

PRIDE OF FLANDERS Flanders is the area of Belgium in which Zeebrugge lies.

PRIDE OF KENT Kent is the county in which Dover is situated.

PRIDE OF RATHLIN Rathlin Island is a small inhabited island off County Antrim, north of Larne.

PRIDE OF SUFFOLK Suffolk is the county in which Felixstowe lies.

PRIDE OF WINCHESTER Winchester is a cathedral city, 21 miles north west of Portsmouth.

PRINS ALBERT Belgian King, born 1934, brother of late King Baudouin I. Succeeded him in 1993.

PRINS FILIP Belgian Prince, born 1960. Son of King Albert. More commonly known in Britain by the French version of his name 'Philippe'.

PURBECK Area to south west of Poole.

QUIBERON Peninsula and small town in south western Brittany.

RAASAY Island to north east of Skye.

REINE ASTRID Belgian Queen, born in Sweden in 1905; died 1935. Wife of King Leopold III who abdicated in 1950 and mother of current Belgian King, Filip/Philippe I.

RHUM Small Inner Hebridean island. Alternative (and older) spelling 'Rum' now used by *Caledonian MacBrayne* in timetables following representations by the islanders.

RIVER LUNE River rising in the Pennines and reaching the sea near Lancaster.

ROSEHAUGH Rosehaugh House is situated on the Black Isle, about 5 miles north east of North Kessock, Inverness, where the vessel originally operated.

SAINT KILLIAN II Seventh century Irish monk who was a missionary in Artois, France.

SAINT PATRICK II Patron Saint of Ireland, c390-c460. Reputedly born in Britain and abducted to Ireland at the age of 16. By the time of his death he had firmly established Christianity in Ireland.

SATURN Roman god of agriculture and father of the gods. Also sixth planet of the solar system.

SHAPINSAY One of the Orkney Islands.

SOUND OF GIGHA Area of sea between Gigha and the Kintyre peninsula.

SOUND OF SANDA Area of sea between Sanda Island and the Kintyre peninsula.

SOUND OF SCARBA Area of sea between Island of Scarba and Scottish mainland.

SOUND OF SEIL Area of sea between the Island of Seil and the Scottish mainland.

SOUND OF SHUNA Area of sea between the islands of Luing and Shuna.

SOUND OF SLEAT Area of sea between south end of Skye and mainland.

ST CATHERINE Fourth Century Christian from Alexandria, reputedly martyred on a spiked wheel. There is a Church dedicated to this saint on the Isle of Wight and the southern-most tip of the island is called St Catherine's Point.

ST CECILIA Second or third century Roman girl who was martyred for her faith. Patron saint of musicians. There is a Benedictine convent dedicated to this saint on the Isle of Wight.

ST CLAIR Alternately 'St Clarus'. Ninth Century native of Rochester, Kent, who became a hermit in France.

ST FAITH Virgin martyr who suffered for her faith at Agen in Aquitaine, France. Died C287. There is a church dedicated to St Faith in Cowes, Isle of Wight.

ST HELEN Roman empress (c248-328), mother of Constantine the Great. There is a Church dedicated to this saint on the Isle of Wight (actually called 'St Helena'). There is also a village called 'St Helens' on the Island.

ST OLA Also known as 'St Olaf'. Born in 995, he became King of Norway in 1016 and Christianised the nation. Deposed in 1029, he was killed in battle in 1030. Patron Saint of Norway.

ST ROGNVALD Earl of Orkney, died 1158 or 1159. Started the building of Kirkwall Cathedral.

ST SUNNIVA Legendary tenth century Irish princess who fled her country and, after being shipwrecked off the Norwegian coast, was murdered on Selje Island.

STENA ANTRIM Antrim is the county in Northern Ireland in which Larne is situated.

STENA CALEDONIA 'Caledonia' was the Roman name for Scotland.

STENA CAMBRIA 'Cambria' was the Roman name for Wales (Note: CAMBRIA and HIBERNIA (see below) were traditional names for Holyhead – Dun Laoghaire railway steamers).

STENA GALLOWAY Galloway is the region in South Western Scotland in which Stranraer is situated.

STENA GOTHICA The Goths were a Germanic tribe who invaded the Roman Empire. Gothic is a style of architecture which developed in the middle ages, whose opponents at the time of the Renaissance dubbed it 'Gothic' as a term of abuse, implying it was barbarian.

STENA HIBERNIA 'Hibernia' was the Roman name for Ireland.

STENA INVICTA 'Invicta' is Latin for 'unconquered', the motto of the county of Kent. Contrary to a common misconception, it is **not** the name of the white horse, which appears above it in the emblem of Kent.

SUILVEN Mountain in Sutherland.

SYMPHORINE Symphoricarpos name of a small flowering shrub.

THE PRINCESS ANNE Daughter of Queen Elizabeth II of the UK, born 1950.

THE PRINCESS MARGARET Sister of Queen Elizabeth II of the UK, born 1930.

THORA Norwegian (and British) girl's name.

THORSVOE Norse name for Mill Bay, Longhope, South Walls, Orkney.

TOR FLANDRIA See PRIDE OF FLANDERS.

TOR GOTHIA See STENA GOTHICA.

UNDINE Water nymph of European legend. Subject of opera by Hoffmann.

VARAGEN Norse word meaning 'our own'.

VENUS Second planet of the solar system and Roman goddess of love.

WINSTON CHURCHILL British statesman. Prime Minister 1940-1945 and 1951-1955.

Glenachulish (Nick Widdows)

Ferry Publications

Ferry Publications was formed in 1987 by Miles Cowsill and John Hendy who had joined together to write and publish their highly successful 'Townsend Thoresen Years'. Since then they have produced a continuous stream of titles which have covered most areas of the North Sea, English Channel and Irish Sea.

Disenchantment with writing for other magazines led the partners to launch their own quarterly journal 'British Ferry Scene' in the Summer of 1989. Now a firmly established favourite, the magazine has quickly gained praise from both the enthusiast fraternity and the ferry industry alike.

BIBLIOGRAPHY

FERRY PUBLICATIONS BOOKS CURRENTLY AVAILABLE

Title	Author(s)	Date
British Channel Island Ferries	Miles Cowsill	1989
Brittany Ferries 1973-1993	Miles Cowsill	1994
By Road Across the Sea (Atlantic Steam Navigation)	Miles Cowsill	1990
Caledonian MacBrayne, The fleet	Cowsill, Hendy & MacDuff	1994
Dover – Ostend Line, The	John Hendy	1991
Earl William (History of Thoresen & Sealink ferry)	Miles Cowsill & John Hendy	1990
Fantasia (Stena Sealink Ferry)	John Hendy	1990
Ferries from Pembrokeshire (2nd edition)	Miles Cowsill	1993
Ferries in Camera '90		1990
Ferries of Dover	John Hendy	1994
Ferries of Scotland (2nd edition)	Miles Cowsill & John Hendy	1994
Ferries of the English Channel	Miles Cowsill & John Hendy	1993
Fishguard – Rosslare	Miles Cowsill	1990
Folkestone – Boulogne 1843-1991 (3rd edition)	John Hendy	1991
Harwich – Hoek van Holland	Cowsill, Hendy & Haalmeijer	1993
Hoverspeed Story, The (2nd edition)	Miles Cowsill & John Hendy	1993
King Orry	Miles Cowsill & John Hendy	1992
Olau (2nd edition)	Miles Cowsill & John Hendy	1990
P&O European Ferries, The fleet (2nd edition)	Miles Cowsill & John Hendy	1992
Saint Germain (Vintage train ferry)	John Hendy	1990
Sally Line	Geoffrey Breeze	1990
Sealink Stena Line, The fleet	Miles Cowsill & John Hendy	1992
Steam Packet Memories	John Shepherd	1993
Townsend Thoresen Years, The (2nd edition)	Miles Cowsill & John Hendy	1987
Viking Saga, The (Cherbourg & Le Havre)	Miles Cowsill & John Hendy	1989
Wightlink (Isle of Wight ferries)	John Hendy	1993
Winston Churchill	Miles Cowsill & John Hendy	1991

OTHER BOOKS

Name	Author	Publisher & Date
Across the Irish Sea	Robert C Sinclair	Conway Maritime Press, London EC4, 1990.
Century of Cross Channel Passenger Ferries, A	Ambrose Greenway	Ian Allan, Shepperton, Middlesex 1981
Century of North Sea Passenger Ferries, A	Ambrose Greenway	Ian Allan, Shepperton, Middlesex 1986
Channel Islands Railway Steamers	K Le Scelleur	Patrick Stephens, Wellingborough, 1985
Clyde River and Other Steamers (4th Edition)	C L D Duckworth & G E Langmuir	Brown, Son and Ferguson, Glasgow, 1990
DFDS 1866-1991	Søren Thorsvø and others	DFDS/World Ship Society, Gravesend, Kent, 1991.
Eight Decades of Heysham Douglas	A M Goodwyn	Manx Electric Rly Soc, Douglas, IOM 1985
Ferries around Britain	John F Hendy	Ian Allan, Shepperton, Middlesex 1985
Fred. Olsen/Bergen Line	N L Middlemiss	Shield Publications Ltd, Newcastle, Tyne & Wear, 1990.
Free for all (Woolwich Free Ferry)	Julian Watson & Wendy Gregory	Greenwich Libraries, Greenwich, 1989
Hebridean and Clyde Ferries of Caledonian MacBrayne	Ian McCrorie	Caledonian MacBrayne, Gourock, 1986
Island Lifeline (Isle of Man Steam Packet Co)	Connery Chappell	T Stephenson & Sons, Prescot, Merseyside 1980
Merchant Fleets (Britain's Railway Steamers) (E, NW, Zeeland & Stena)	Duncan Haws	TCL Publications, Hereford 1993
Merchant Fleets (Britain's Railway Steamers) (W, S, French & Stena)	Duncan Haws	TCL Publications, Hereford 1993
Lymington – The Sound of Success	Alan Brown	Alan T Condie Publications, Nuneaton, 1988.

Newhaven-Dieppe	B M E O'Mahoney	Capella Publications, Stowmarket, Suffolk 1980
Night Ferry	G Behrend & G Buchanan	Jersey Artists, Jersey 1985
North Sea Ferries – Ships of the Night	Barry Mitchell	Coastline Press, Bridlington, N Yorks 1991
Papenburg Sisters, The	Geoffrey Breeze	Kingfisher Railway Productions, Southampton 1986
Red Funnel and Before	R B Adams	Kingfisher Railway Productions, Southampton 1986
Sealink	Brian Haresnape	Ian Allan, Shepperton, Middlesex 1982
Short Sea Route, The (Stranraer-Larne)	Fraser G MacHaffie	T Stephenson & Sons, Prescot, Merseyside 1975
Speed Bonny Boat (Caledonian MacBrayne 1969-1990)	John Whittle	Saltire Communications, Edinburgh 1990
Steamers of the Highlands and Islands	Ian McCrorie	Orr, Pollock & Co, Greenock 1987
Super-ferries of Britain, Europe & Scandinavia	Russell Plummer	Patrick Stephens, Europe and Wellingborough 1988
To the Coast	Ian McCrorie	The Fairlie Press, Fairlie, Ayrshire, 1989.
West Highland Steamers (4th Edition)	C L D Duckworth & G E Langmuir	Brown, Son and Ferguson, Glasgow, 1987
Worldwide High Speed Ferries	Paul Hynds	Conway Maritime Press, London EC4, 1992

REGULAR PUBLICATIONS

Monthly

Cruising Monthly	Coastal Cruising Association, 48 Brookshall Road IPSWICH, Suffolk IP1 4BZ	A
Sea Breezes	Jocast Ltd, 202 Cotton Exchange Buildings Old Hall Street, LIVERPOOL L3 9LA	B
Ships Monthly	Waterway Publications, Kottingham House Dale Street, BURTON ON TRENT, Staffs DE14 3TD	B

Quarterly

| British Ferry Scene | Ferry Publications, 12 Millfields Close
Pentlepoir, KILGETTY, Pembs SA68 0SA | C |

Annual

| Guide | Plus 2 Ferryconsultation, PO Box 7067
S-300 07, HALMSTAD, Sweden | D |

| Designs | Plus 2 Ferryconsultation (as above) | D |

Bi-annual

| Trip out | G P Hamer, 77 St Mary's Grove, LONDON W4 3LW | E |

Notes

A – This newsletter is provided for members of the CCA as part of their subscription; the address shown is that of the publicity officer to whom membership enquiries should be directed. Despite the name, about 80% of it is devoted to ferry news. B – These are two national ship enthusiast magazines, covering all aspects of shipping. Both have regular ferry news columns plus occasional articles on ferry topics. C – This is the only magazine devoted solely to ferries and is produced to Ferry Publications' normal high standards. D – This is published in English to a very high standard. 'Guide' is a world list of ferries, cruise liners and freight RO/ROs and 'Designs' features recently delivered vessels. Aimed primarily at the shipping industry, it is rather expensive but special rates are available for 'bona fide' enthusiasts who agree to purchase both publications. E – Over 900 passenger vessels listed on a geographical basis.

INDEX

DANA ANGLIA	40	JAMES NEWMAN	81
DANA CIMBRIA	86	JOHN BURNS	81
DANA CORONA	86	JUNO	60
DANA MAXIMA	86	JUPITER	60
DUC DE NORMANDIE	12	KING ORRY	20
DUCHESSE ANNE	12	KJELLA	76
EARL SIGURD	69	KOADA	76
EARL THORFINN	69	KONINGIN BEATRIX	44
EGLANTINE	84	LADY OF MANN	20
EIGG	60	LAXFOSS	88
EILEAN BHEARNARAIGH	80	LEIRNA	76
EILEAN NA H-OIGE	80	LOCH BUIE	60
ELK	98	LOCH DUNVEGAN	60
EMERAUDE	54	LOCH FYNE	60
ERNEST BEVIN	81	LOCH LINNHE	60
EUROPEAN CLEARWAY	100	LOCH RANZA	60
EUROPEAN ENDEAVOUR	97	LOCH RIDDON	60
EUROPEAN FREEWAY	97	LOCH STRIVEN	60
EUROPEAN HIGHWAY	97	LOCH TARBERT	60
EUROPEAN PATHWAY	97	LOCHMOR	60
EUROPEAN SEAWAY	97	LORD OF THE ISLES	60
EUROPEAN TIDEWAY	97	LOVERVAL	84
EUROPEAN TRADER	97	LYONESSE LADY	66
EYNHALLOW	69	MAERSK FLANDERS	94
F.B.D. DUNBRODY	72	MAID OF GLENCOUL	66
FICHTELBERG	86	MERCHANT BRAVERY	93
FIESTA	41	MERCHANT BRILLIANT	93
FILLA	76	MERCHANT VALIANT	100
FIVLA	76	MERCHANT VENTURE	93
FYLGA	76	MISNEACH	58
GABRIELE WEHR	97	MORVERN	60
GEIRA	76	NETLEY CASTLE	73
GLENACHULISH	65	NORBANK	96
GLENBROOK	64	NORBAY	96
GOOD SHEPHERD IV	76	NORCAPE	96
GRIMA	76	NORD PAS-DE-CALAIS	102
GRY MARITHA	66	NORDBORG	84
HAMBURG	40	NORKING	96
HAVELET	17	NORLAND	25
HEBRIDEAN ISLES	60	NORMAN COMMODORE	85
HENDRA	76	NORMANDIE	12
HENRY STAHL	105	NORMANDIE SHIPPER	104
HOVERSPEED GREAT BRITAIN	56	NORQUEEN	96
HOY HEAD	69	NORRIS CASTLE	73
HOY HEAD II	69	NORSE LAGAN	21
INOWROCLAW	89	NORSE MERSEY	21
IONA	60	NORSEA	25
ISLE OF ARRAN	60	NORSKY	96
ISLE OF CUMBRAE	60	NORSTAR	25
ISLE OF INISHMORE	10	NORSUN	25
ISLE OF INNISFREE	10	OLAU BRITANNIA	25
ISLE OF MULL	60	OLAU HOLLANDIA	25

PEVERIL	92	SOUND OF SCARBA	79
PIONEER	60	SOUND OF SEIL	79
PORTAFERRY FERRY	65	SOUND OF SHUNA	79
PRIDE OF AILSA	32	SOUND OF SLEAT	79
PRIDE OF BILBAO	32	SPHEROID	82
PRIDE OF BRUGES	32	SPIRIT OF BOULOGNE	93
PRIDE OF BURGUNDY	32	ST CATHERINE	81
PRIDE OF CALAIS	32	ST CECILIA	81
PRIDE OF CHERBOURG	32	ST CLAIR	70
PRIDE OF DOVER	32	ST FAITH	81
PRIDE OF FLANDERS	32	ST HELEN	81
PRIDE OF HAMPSHIRE	32	ST OLA	70
PRIDE OF KENT	32	ST ROGNVALD	100
PRIDE OF LE HAVRE	32	ST SUNNIVA	70
PRIDE OF RATHLIN	32	STENA ANTRIM	45
PRIDE OF SUFFOLK	32	STENA CALEDONIA	45
PRIDE OF WINCHESTER	32	STENA CAMBRIA	45
PRINCE OF SCANDINAVIA	40	STENA CHALLENGER	45
PRINCESS OF SCANDINAVIA	40	STENA EUROPE	44
PRINCESSE MARIE-CHRISTINE	29	STENA FANTASIA	45
PRINS ALBERT	29	STENA FELICITY	45
PRINS FILIP	29	STENA GALLOWAY	45
PUMA	100	STENA GOTHICA	103
PURBECK	85	STENA HIBERNIA	45
QUIBERON	12	STENA INVICTA	45
RAASAY	60	STENA LONDONER	45
RED FALCON	73	STENA NORMANDY	45
REINE ASTRID	29	STENA PARISIEN	45
RHUM	60	STENA SEA LYNX	57
RIVER LUNE	82	STENA SEATRADER	44
ROSEANNE	94	STRANGFORD FERRY	65
ROSEHAUGH	66	SUILVEN	60
SAGA MOON	82	SUPERFERRY	52
SAINT KILLIAN II	21	SYMPHORINE	84
SAINT PATRICK II	21	THE PRINCESS ANNE	56
SALLY EUROBRIDGE	96	THE PRINCESS MARGARET	56
SALLY EUROLINK	101	THORA	76
SALLY EUROROUTE	101	THORSVOE	69
SALLY SKY	36	TOR ANGLIA	103
SALLY STAR	36	TOR BRITANNIA	103
SALLY SUN	101	TOR CALEDONIA	103
SATURN	60	TOR DANIA	86
SCILLONIAN III	66	TOR FLANDRIA	103
SEACAT BOULOGNE	56	TOR GOTHIA	103
SEACAT CALAIS	56	TOR HOLLANDIA	103
SEACAT SCOTLAND	56	UNDINE	84
SHANNON HEATHER	73	VAL DE LOIRE	12
SHANNON WILLOW	73	VARAGEN	69
SHAPINSAY	69	VENUS	16
SMYRIL	49	VIKING TRADER	100
SOLIDOR 2	17	WINSTON CHURCHILL	40
SOUND OF GIGHA	78		